RESULTS
DO
MATTER

**A Journey from
Homeless
to Million-Dollar
Business Success**

JAMES GULLATTE

Results Do Matter: A Journey from Homeless to Million-Dollar Business Success
Copyright 2020 by James Gullatte

B.O.S.S. Fitness
333 E. Livingston Ave.
Columbus, Ohio 43215
www.boss-fitness.com

Publisher's Cataloging-In-Publication Data
(Prepared by The Donohue Group, Inc.)

Names: Gullatte, James, author.
    Title: Results do matter : journey from homeless to million-dollar
    business success / James Gullatte.
Description: [Columbus, Ohio] : B.O.S.S. Fitness, [2020]
Identifiers: ISBN 9781734778205 (paperback) I ISBN 9781734778212
    (hardcover) I ISBN 9781734778229 (ebook)
Subjects: LCSH: Gullatte, James. I African American businesspeople--Ohio--
    Biography. I African American homeless persons--Ohio--Biography. I
    Personal trainers--Ohio--Biography. I Success in business. I LCGFT:
    Autobiographies.
Classification: LCC HC102.5.G85 A3 2020 (print) I LCC HC102.5.G85 (ebook)
    I DDC 338.092--dc23

This is a work of creative nonfiction. Events are portrayed to the best of the author's memory. All the stories in this book are true to the author's recollection although some names and identifying details have been changed to protect the privacy of the individuals involved.

To the kid who is where I was—lost, on the streets, in poverty. May you make it out, too. Let my story inspire you. Results do matter.

Table of Contents

PART I:
Early Years

Eulogy

Man, how do I start? James, AKA Master Trainer James, the Motivator, the Inspiration, the Energizer Bunny! All that knew him can back this up. And to go even deeper, James was a guy who would bend over backward for you if you were in his circle. To his own fault, James's biggest gift was also his biggest downfall. He always saw the good in others. Because of his travels, he would always believe you when you said you wanted something. Once he buys into your story, he will push you, challenge you, and offer up any support he can whether it be through connections of his, money out his pocket, or just to come sit with you and encourage you. James doesn't back off. He will not allow anyone around him to be without accountability for the things they say out their mouth.

Something I so admire about James is he held himself accountable for his actions. How many folks do you know can actually do what they say they are going to do? If you know him closely enough for him to open up to you, the one thing you will find is he never makes excuses for his place in life. He doesn't allow any situation to keep him from his goals.

As a juvenile, James spent time in and out of juvenile detention centers. He stayed on this path into adulthood, ending up in prison for ten years. That is when the light bulb came on, and his journey began to take meaning. He created B.O.S.S. Fitness for the sole purpose of saving his life and bringing his family back together. James wanted to be a mentor to men. When he said B.O.S.S. Fitness is more than recreation, but a way of life, he *meant* it.

B.O.S.S. literally saved his life. His energy came from this; he wanted to spread his fitness to as many people as possible and do so with a high level of integrity. Some believe James is very passionate, controlling, and very demanding . . . this is true! I will tell you this much—James is very for real. If B.O.S.S. Fitness could save the life of such a lost soul, what could it do for someone else? James can make you smile when your day isn't going well. James can also find a way to piss you the heck off. The one thing you cannot say about James is he doesn't care. He cares about people. If he doesn't like you, you know it.

For such a complex person, he is really simple. James is straightforward, dependable, reliable, consistent, caring, honest, focused, and a hard worker. James is not someone who quits. James takes life by the balls and gives it the middle finger. James calls bullshit on you quick!

James is a very aggressive person, very determined. After being homeless, left behind by your friends and family, doing ten years in prison only to get out and still be homeless for twelve years, you might be just as aggressive and determined. After these experiences, James knew what he wanted. Sometimes people did not understand what he was saying or doing, but you better believe James was trying to figure it out. Underneath the protectiveness, the aggression, the passion, the fire, the energy, the motivation, and don't forget the money! James is an awesome guy. He loves hard, and if you are in this room today, he has shared some form of his love with you . . . the James way. In closing, like my James would say . . . I got the eye of the tiger, lion-headed through the fire! Because I am a champion, and you're going to hear me roar.

Prelude

I am currently sitting in the day room of North Central Correctional Facility finishing out a ten-year sentence. With fifty-six days left before being let back into society, I have many thoughts running through my mind. For so long, I've considered how it would feel to finally know when I can go home. Prison life is basically all I can remember about my manhood. Before entering this facility, I didn't have one idea of what a man could be.

Even in my present condition, I was able to create this vision of my life and how I'd like it to be. Being incarcerated doesn't mean it's simple to change. Yes, reality does stare you in the eye day in and day out. But having the actual courage and willingness to be honest with yourself, and then assess what you find, that's a very tough situation.

I guess one of the problems is we have so much time to think that we can overthink, or we can underthink, or we can just accept the reality that we find. Because of the abnormal conditions we live under, false expectations are being made daily. We're talking about 2,000 men of mixed ages and genders, from different backgrounds, with one thing in common: jail.

This portion of my life was not by chance. If you believe in things happening for a reason, then the trials I faced were only to bring me to the point I've reached today. The same adversities we face in the process of changing in society, we face in prison. The only problem about changing in prison is that no one believes you, and the years are some of the loneliest times you will face.

I hear people talking about programs to help improve a person's current condition. In prison, out of 2,000 men, only a small percentage even attend the programs they have to offer. Society looks at the recidivism rate and thinks every man or woman coming out of these places is the same. What society doesn't get to see is how many convicted felons spend their time.

In the day room, you will have a room full of intelligent men sharing their viewpoints on how life is, whether it's their own or somebody like Jennifer Lopez's. In the day room, you will hear a great plan of how some guy who drinks three types of Kool Aid, coffee, and Jolly Ranchers mixed, calling it a Foxy, is going to get rich. He spends all his time playing cards or board games. He watches TV and gossips about everybody else's business, and yet he could tell you how to get your life together.

The sad thing about this is there are prisons full of guys who define themselves through alter egos, which change with each sport. And since every other person in prison has some size, you can imagine the testosterone battles after each recreational period. So changing is a big step for the convicted felon behind bars, and it's even harder when they're let back into society. Just like the man or woman who has to wake up every day, go to work, and find ways to provide for his or her family, folks in prison are doing the same thing. We have to work or go to school and providing for our family is always on our mind.

This book is about some of my experiences with the hope that I can be an inspiration to someone. I do not profess to have been through something no one else has. Frankly, I've experienced the same type of pitfalls as every other black urban youth. It's a known fact that many of my fellow peers don't make it out of the street life unscathed. Most young hustlers become old hustlers. The illusion that hustling is cool is widespread, and to a ton of people, the game is their reality. It was my reality up until I received this ten-year sentence.

Whether you are on the streets hustling every day, or in an office building, the same criticisms face you. Pressure is maybe the leading cause of irrational decision-making. Under pressure, we will make choices we would not normally make. It's sad, but true. We often believe once we are spiraling down, there is no stopping us. The saying *If you do it once, you will do it again* is a lie. Many of us lack the courage to make the necessary changes in our lives to prevent repeating bad actions. And when you combine the lack of direction with the lack of courage, then you get repeat offenders.

My present condition dictates how my actions later in life will be. Evolving out of low self-esteem, which plagues so many of my fellow peers, takes me down a path of acceptance and reluctance. I need to accept my position as a man of God, father, son, and everything I've been placed on this Earth to be. This newly attained attitude leaves me looking at life in a whole different light. Of course, my old habits are constantly trying to ease their way back into my life.

A powerful speaker once said that when we become new, the enemy within is constantly trying to fight its way out. The amusing part of this statement is he called the enemy *Jason*. Jason was hard to kill. Every time you got him down, the man would pop right back up. The first step is always easy, but the second step takes dedication, determination, and a lot of focus.

Throughout my youth, every chance anyone got to speak words of encouragement to me, they did. The problem with that is they often lied to me. In telling a young child he can do anything he puts his mind to, you leave the door open for a lot of letdowns.

Everybody can't do the same things their mind is telling them to do.

Instead of someone taking the time out to help me find my niche, they fed me a lot of stories, pep talks, and occasionally some money. Being naïve, I believed these things meant a person cared. But if they did, why did I feel so alone?

In any event, I spent the majority of my life abusing or amusing myself with meaningless relationships, an excessive use of drugs, and a great deal of trouble. For twenty-five years, the biggest illusion in my young life was believing I loved myself.

If asked the question, "Do you love yourself?" I would answer with an emphatic "Yes" until I had an honest conversation with myself. I asked myself, "If you love yourself, why are you sitting in prison?" My love for myself, at the time, was measured the same way anyone else showed me they loved me: with gifts or praise. At twenty-five, I had seven kids by five different women. And I was in no position to help any of them. I think at this time I had this epiphany: I didn't want to end up like my father. He had walked away from his responsibilities and left my mom to try and raise a boy into a man. It was time to turn my life around. And the first step was to start caring about myself.

Even at this time, I've given into a lot of open expressions of emotions by getting tattoos, running with a gang, and still trying to make a name for myself. I soon discovered saying you want to change and actually doing it are two very different challenges. Looking back, everything was a process. Many times, throwing the towel in was the only option. At my weakest point, when it seemed like there was no other option but to give up, the fire deep down inside of me that gives me the desire to want to live starts to burn a little stronger.

Did you know you can secretly defeat yourself by not utilizing all the tools, gifts, and talents given to you by the creator? Instead of using the fact that I didn't have a high school diploma to push myself, I used it as an excuse to deceive myself. And deceiving myself is just what I did for many years.

It wasn't until the biggest deception of them all hit me smack dead in the face. I was really and truly alone. The parole board served me with another five years. At the time, I had only served four years. My great talents of manipulation, deception, and many other learned bad characteristics and mannerisms had gotten me nowhere. In jail with no one to call, no one to write, and no visits, I realized that the only person to blame for my conditions was myself. And this is when the change became imminent. So I guess the breaking point, my bottom, came after being in prison for four years.

The start of this book began during my incarceration, and at this point, I'm on my tenth and god-willing, last year. Even behind these fences and metal doors, my dreams continue to soar. My hope is alive, and the vision is right there. Being in a place where you wake up to the reality of who you are on a daily basis is not easy. For the determined one, reality takes a new meaning. So many of my peers seek a life of prosperity. Yes, unrealistic dreams are formed. But tell me, what would you expect coming from a bunch of socioeconomically deprived and underdeveloped men?

On that same note, I had to believe I could become a better person. My quest was to find out who I really was, then turn him into somebody. Unbeknownst to me, I was already somebody, just not somebody that I liked.

I have to say, prison is where my life began to make sense. Believe it or not, you do have a choice whether to dwell in your past or move toward the type of life you really want. Coming from a single-parent home in a rough financial situation, my experiences led to many not-so-good outcomes. I truly believe that until a person has reached a breaking point in their life, they will continue to repeat the same cycle that caused them so much pain. When your confidence is down and the feeling of being alone keeps beating at your heart, how do you get motivated? The answers to anyone's problems are all within.

Little Junior

Junior was the naïve little boy who really didn't understand what was going on around him, but for some reason, he knew something was missing. Despite not knowing who his father was for the majority of his early years, things still seemed OK. My parents divorced when I was one. After the breakup, my mom wouldn't allow him to come around, and he didn't try to come around either.

It could have been an easy four- to five-year span between me seeing my father to me seeing him again. This may not be accurate, but from my memory, it's right on time. I often wondered why my father named me after him, but never treated me like a son. Because of my first name, Horace, Junior seemed more appealing. Majority of my earlier fights as a youth were instigated by jokes about my name. If you know kids, then you know I fought often.

I believe the fights stemmed from the name-calling, but later in life, I learned the fights were about not having my father around. He gave me this funny name to make himself proud, but he was not there to show me how to defend myself or to teach me how to act like a little boy is supposed to act. Remember, I was still very young and not understanding how all this was affecting me.

My mom used to tell me stories about my father, and none of them were good. She would always tell me I was her man and the man of the house, so it became my responsibility to take care of my mother and sister. My mom would have boyfriends, because she was still young herself. But the only thing that registered to me was if I am her man, then what is this man doing sleeping over and telling my mom what to do?

There was one boyfriend or two who were kind of cool. Scott, he was cool. He and my mom lasted for a little while. Scott is one of them slick dudes, though. He worked a nice job, but he played the field. I remember him and my mom getting into it over his supposed ex-girlfriend a couple times. Scott's family was OK. They accepted us like their own until my mom and Scott broke up.

Then there was this one guy named Dee. He was kind of too young for my mom, but she didn't know I knew this. Dee would try and help me learn how to read and play ball with me sometimes, but still, he wasn't my dad. I believe Dee was the one I had to pull my baseball bat on and let him know who the real man of the house was.

Between the boyfriends and the other mess going on, my father started coming back around. The first time I met my father was over at my Aunt Trudy's house. Aunt Trudy was the big sister and second in charge. If I was in trouble with my mom, I would call my aunt and cry to her and the punishment could get lifted. Aunt Trudy was four feet eleven inches and mean. Everybody feared Aunt Trudy, so meeting my father there was the neutral point.

I was so excited to be seeing my father for the first time. The doorbell rang. I ran to the door, opened it up, called my uncle Butch, and yelled, "My daddy here." Man, it wasn't even my dad, it was my uncle's friend. He didn't even know us. Man, that was weird. A little while later, my Pops showed up, and we talked for a while. After that point, he started coming over every now and then, bringing gifts and money, but never spending any time. Matter of fact, his car never got turned off.

It was my dad who introduced me to baseball by buying me a baseball bat, glove, and ball for my birthday. I was the only one in the neighborhood with one, so every time the kids played ball, I had to play. This is how I got good and found my first love for anything other than my mother.

The years that went by without seeing my father, I think it was because we were hiding from him. My grandfather was looking for him for a little bit too. We started out in public housing, the Summer Square. This is where I learned to fight and how to duck. The ducking came after I didn't duck, and some girl hit me with a slap-scratch down my face. It was a scar which still stands to this day. By the way, I was being mannish, and I touched her on the butt. You know the rest.

The Adams were a permanent fixture in the square. They had this big family who lived all over the square. Momma Adams used to babysit my sister and me while my mom was at work. Her sons Tommy and Roddy were older than us, but were still around the same age. They would play jokes on me like fix peanut butter and jelly sandwiches, then send me to wash my hands. After washing my hands, I would come back, and they'd say, "Let's play this game; let's open up our sandwiches." When I would open my sandwich, a fly would be in mine. I couldn't cry, because that would make them hit me and laugh at me. Tommy was kind of my dude because he was bad.

Tommy would make me fight every little dude my age in the square. There were two little dudes who got smart on me and started waiting until Tommy wasn't around, and they would jump on me, run my butt home. My mom would make me go right back out there and fight.

Summer Square was just a pit stop because we soon moved into a house up in the suburbs. This move didn't last too long either. While there, I met a few buddies who liked to fight and run things. In the suburbs at this time, it may be three guys who could fight, and even less who would. Being the littlest one in the bunch, I had a larger status because I would fight. This is about the time the fixation of becoming a daredevil kicked in. My first try at this led me to get six stitches across the forehead.

A couple years out in the suburbs, and things started happening. My mom lost her good job because she was trying to play the system, then my grandfather sprung for a house for us. The house was back in the hood. Our first day there was different. I had never seen kids hang out in the streets. These kids ran up on us like we already knew them. My sister didn't mind much because it was mostly boys.

Things ran a whole lot different in West Wood than they did in Jefferson Township or Summer Square. All hours of the night, people hung out if the weather permitted. Plus, these kids stole stuff from the neighborhood store. It didn't take me long to fit right in with the rest of the crew.

We stayed in the house for about one year before my mom decided she wanted to live in California. On the summer break in 1982, we packed up our bags and headed for the sunny state. When we got there, we stayed with a friend of my mom's in the city of El Monte. This was a predominately Hispanic town at the time. And in the complex we lived in, there were only three black families. We couldn't wear red, and we couldn't use certain words. While there, we visited many of the beaches.

My mom and I, we used to go over to Oakland and visit a friend of hers. Everything was good for a moment. My mom was working, my sister and I were making friends. My mom and her friend started having problems with each other, and before you knew it, we were living in Englewood.

This was straight for the eye to see. The lady we stayed with gave strict orders to me and my sister to only play in the yard. Early in the morning, we could walk together up to the donut palace and straight back. You could hear gunshots and music all hours of the day and night. Mrs: Earnestine used to throw her own parties also. My mom was stressing out over our situation, but she was still trying.

At one of the parties, I saw my first man-on-man activity. It really blew my mind, because I didn't know much about that, but I knew it had to be wrong.

Mrs. Earnestine's son was twenty-one or something. He took me to every baseball stadium in California to see a game. He would take me to the gym, and we'd do stuff like that.

One day my mom woke up, and she had had enough. She packed up the Chevette, collected her last check, and we were on our way back to Ohio just in time to start another school year. While in California, my mom rented the house to a friend of hers. By arriving unannounced like we did, we had to stay with yet another friend until our house was ready.

After finally getting back into our house and back around my boys, the whole experience had taken its toll on me. It was at this point my life started taking a turn for the worst. Somehow, I had started losing respect for my mother and resenting her for her choices. I believed her attempt to introduce male figures in my life were only attempts at her own happiness, which always had the same outcome.

I was a normal kid getting into trouble but still went to school and got OK grades and played sports. By this time at the baseball park, my skills were being rewarded by trips with the all-star team and traveling throughout Ohio to play. My thirteen-year-old all-star team nearly made it to a game at Williamsport, Pennsylvania, the Little League World Series. I remember my days playing and making a good play and leading my team to a win with not one family member in the stands. All the cheers came from my teammates' parents. They must have felt some pity for me, because they would pick me up and take me home. Buy me stuff for baseball, little things.

One year my father came to one game and was yelling the regular "That's my boy" stuff. The other parents had a look on their faces. My father never came to another game. At fourteen, baseball, basketball, football were still a part of my life. My grades were still good but added to the equation were girls, gangs, drinking, smoking weed, and another type of attention. By not receiving attention at home and from my family, I sought other means to fulfill what was missing.

Soon my grades started slipping, I started stealing clothes and shoes. I even started getting play from the top girls in the class. I joined a gang called the Young Dawgs. Mostly because my friends were in it. We did the things that gangs do and received a lot of trouble and a lot of attention for it.

Being a part of the Young Dawgs brought respect that I don't believe any of us expected. The reputation of the gang, which started with three members, spread like wildfire. Before we all knew it, our personal reputations were growing, and it was my pleasure to keep mine growing. At this time, my mom had no idea that these things were happening. I would go out, rob, steal, drink, smoke, fight, disrespect grownups, and be home by 11:00. Sometimes things would happen that told me I really wasn't so tough. I had things my friends didn't have.

Being the youngest of the kids, everybody kind of spoiled me. There were times my mom wouldn't let her feelings toward my father, or the complications of her own life, get in the way of showing me how much she loved me. During these times, I felt being involved in the things I was involved with didn't make any sense. Despite being a very intelligent young man, I was terribly naïve to the inner workings of survival. We always had food, a place to stay, and heat. Even with the signs and the sometimes family moments, there was something deep down in me. It was like a hole in my life.

After the summer of '84 when the Young Dogs managed to establish themselves in the streets, many of us went back to school with more experience as young men and a lot of people who did not care for us. For me, this was the year I stepped it up with the ladies. Let's just say, my ninth-grade year is when I lost my virginity. Prior to this moment, I had only told lies about having sex. There was occasional kissing and touching, but nothing like the first time.

Also, this year the schools were realigned, and the Atomic Dog boys were getting bused over to school with us. Not many of our crew had experience being sent to juvenile detention, but that was soon to change. A close friend of mine who I grew up with because our moms were friends and our grandparents lived two doors apart, came over in the new alignment. He was an Atomic Dog.

The year started out real nice. My current girlfriend was a cheerleader, and she was a year younger than me. And we had been going together since the year before. When we came back to school, new things were going on, and I ended up messing around with a girl in my class. This girl was already having sex, or so I heard through the grapevine, and she liked me. She used to come to school with pockets full of quarters and give them to me. Later I found out she was stealing the money from her father, who sold weed.

Kim and I talked for maybe a week or two, and then we started going together. One day, I was hanging with my boy Larry, and he asked me if I was still going out with Kim. And when I said, "Yeah," he started laughing. Then he told me some stuff that had happened.

He told me, "Man, she got Young Dogged."

I'm like, "What?"

He said, "Yeah, man, Lamar had convinced her to come down to the house with him and hang out, and a few of the fellows were there. So she started having sex with Lamar, and while she was having sex with Lamar, all the boys came in the room, and they started feeling her under the cover. "Soon after it got done, Lamar went on his way, and Kim asked him to walk her home and Lamar said, 'No.' So she asked Larry to do it. Larry said, 'I'll walk you home if you give me some.'"

That was my first lesson about women. I didn't care about Kim, but I liked her. I cared about Tisha, my real girlfriend, who wasn't having sex. I never told Kim that I knew what she had done, but I stepped my game up and had to get me some. Once that happened, my life started changing even more. Now that I knew how it felt, there was no stopping me from going after some more.

Sports was still a part of my life, but there were also many other things to keep my mind occupied. A majority of the gang played sports along with me. The only sport we really could play was football, because grades didn't come out until after the season was over. If your GPA dropped too low, you were prohibited from playing sports. Somehow doing schoolwork became very unpopular to a lot of us kids.

Meanwhile, my mom was still trying to hold her life together. She was watching her son get lost into a life she never dreamed of him having. And on top of that, my sister didn't turn out to be the brightest spot in the family either.

My father had another son by another woman. He had long been a part of our family, but now he was living with us too. I was at the point of being grown, tired of being ignored, played, or mistreated because of who my father was. I was doing my own thing but still needed someone to take care of me.

Mom and Dad

My parents were two young people looking to establish a family and grow old together. They met at my mom's work. She was working at a grocery store as a checkout clerk. My dad was an only child and pretty much got everything he wanted. On the outside looking at my father, you wouldn't have known he came from a family of alcoholics and abusers. Meanwhile, my mom was taken aback by this tall, dark, and handsome fellow with a smooth tongue and a nice ride. They started dating, and one thing led to another, and here I am.

Individually they had their fine points, but they were also scarred by the things which took place in their own life. My mom was the baby of her family. Her older sisters really were the ones who took care of her. My grandmother passed away when my mother was fourteen. My aunts were old enough to move out on their own, so once my grandmother died and my grandfather remarried my grandmother's friend, they left the house. Once the new wife came, she brought her own daughter, who was the age of my mother, into the home. In the meantime, Grandpa was drinking heavily and running back and forth to Kentucky with his other family. My mom was catching all kinds of grief from her stepmother because she wasn't hers. Her stepsister had her own phone in her room, got to go places, and had nice things, while my mother had to work for everything she got. Grandpa was busy getting drunk and running around.

Pops acted like he was a gift from God. He was never really disciplined, and every one of his family was a drunk. He had an aunt who loved the boy to her grave. No matter what he did, she

18

always had his back. His father was not around much when he was growing up. I have never met my father's father.

Somewhere between my two dysfunctional parents, a relationship was able to form. My guess would be one was looking for guidance and the other was looking for someone to take care of them.

Pops was really violent. And he couldn't keep his hands off women. In his life, he was a cross between a pimp and a gangster, but with a job. His hatred for women came from the hate he had deep down for his own mother. Even with the bad qualities my father may have had, he remained dedicated and loyal to one woman, but his expectations of this woman were impossible.

Big Horace is what they called my father. He was a tall, good-looking man and a heck of a charmer. If you could take away his resentment toward women, he was just what a man should be. He was hardworking, took care of his home, and spent time with most of his kids. Unfortunately, the kids were spread out among several women, and they all hated him for his abuse, so it was hard for him to spend time with or do the things he could for his kids.

For so long, his story was never heard because there was really no way I could understand his side, because he hurt my mom. The few times as a kid that I spent time with my dad, something would always happen. For instance, my brother Daniel and I were spending the night once and my dad's cousin Spunky lived across the hall. My dad and Spunky were like boys. And they always drank and did things together. Spunky and his wife were over to my dad's apartment playing cards, and an hour after cousin Spunky and his wife left, Pops received a call. His wife wanted my dad to come over; it was an emergency. When we arrived over to Spunk's house, his wife pointed to the back. My brother, my dad, and I, walked together on each other's heels. We could see Spunk's feet on the ground.

My father got there first and turned around to not let Daniel and I see cousin Spunk dead on the ground from a shot to the head.

Another time, Pops took Daniel and me by our little sister's house, and her mother and my dad were having problems. He jumped on her in front of us. Then there was the time when we spent time with his family. When there was drinking, fighting soon followed. My grandmother and her sister got into a fight in front of the kids. There really hasn't been a history of a lot of happy times between us until later on in my life.

Despite the constant drama and his absence, once he came back into my life, birthdays and Christmases, they were done proper. He even took time out for my sister, who was one or two years old when he and my mom met. He actually adopted my sister and gave her his name.

My father passed away January 7, 1999. When he died, he died alone after years of mistreating women in his life. After four or five marriages and tons of relationships, no one was there with him coming down the stretch. They found Pops dead in his apartment by himself. Rest in peace.

His death came from health complications. His body couldn't produce or metabolize the proper nutrients to keep him functioning. He had to get B12 shots once a week to stay going. Out of seven days, he was good for maybe two of them. This condition was a result of being shot by his mother's husband. My grandmother and Pops didn't speak for years afterward. She took her husband's side over her son's. The argument started with drinking. My dad was, at the time, six-feet-two, maybe 220. After being shot and losing 80 percent of his stomach, he shrank to 130.

The doctors ordered him to stop drinking and smoking, because it would eat up to 20 percent of what he had left, but it didn't happen. It ultimately killed him.

My mother, despite all her trials, was a very strong woman. She endured a lonely spirit from losing her mother, which still plagues her today. Coming up, there was never a time I remember my mom giving up. In order to feed her family, she did what she had to do. But she never gave in to the temptations she could have when things got too hard. Instead, she kept her nose to the ground, and she came up with what she needed to do to feed her kids.

She wasn't the type to drink or smoke anything. We never have seen our mother drunk or high. Watching my mother struggle the way she did rubbed off on me. A lot of the things I did early on was to take pressure off her. There was never a chance I would let go by to assist in any of the money problems. The love I had coming up for my mother was that of any little boy running up under his mother.

For a while, we had the type of relationship we were supposed to have. As I got older, our differences became visible. My sister and my mother were close and have a bond that still can't be broken. It's very hard to write about my mother. We've been through so much individually and together that my feelings have been mixed. There are always good logical reasons behind decisions everyone makes in life.

I love my mom so much that it became easy to resent her. I never had big expectations for my Pops, because he crushed those dreams early in my life. When he crushed me, my mom always put the pieces back together. However, I could never really get over the times as a youngster when my mom clearly chose my sister over me. I've been punished for things my sister has done and am constantly reminded of who I am when it comes to them. Of course every decision has justification, but she has never really shared with me why.

Yes, as a child I have done things that maybe should not have been done. I was held to blame for trying to provide myself with what the other children had. And yes, I took for granted that my mother would always be there. Even putting me out of the house consistently from fifteen to eighteen, she never let them keep me when I did get caught stealing or whatever. I don't think there has been forgiveness for the time she told them to just lock me up. I've never been a single mother trying to raise a son by a man I despise. I can't imagine what it feels like to be a scarred woman raising a son who reminds you of so many bad decisions.

With all this said, my mother is still the epitome of the type of woman I want as a life partner. She never went to college, but yet you can't tell. My mom cuts the grass, paints the house, and can still put on a dress and be a lady. There has never been a place she couldn't go. There has never been a place she couldn't get to; there has never been a situation she couldn't get out of. Her heart is big with empathy like no other. My mom is a person of integrity and honor who will not just sell herself because you think she should. In their own way, my parents gave me the best love they could give me. They called me their son, but for real, I was their victim.

Changing

At the age of fifteen, things seemed to be going well. I was in my second ninth grade year and still asleep as to the reason. I wanted to fit in so badly with a certain clique of dudes that them using me never bothered me. We would either come late or not at all. If the principal caught us at the attendance office getting a tardy slip for class, he would just make us leave saying, "Try again tomorrow."

On my second go around with the ninth grade, and they had chosen to send me to an alternative school. The word alternative is used loosely, because this was the last straw. Instead of going to school a full day like normal kids, we went half days, switching between morning sessions or afternoon sessions.

This school was full of drug dealers and gangbangers, all menaces to the public school system. There were also girls who were either pregnant or already had a child. A nursery was in the school also, to allow the teenage mothers a place to take their kids during school. On top of that, there were the ones who were too old to finish high school, so they talked smack to whoever would listen.

A typical day at school would be shooting basketball all morning. Between classes, we would bum rush the store across the street and steal beer and wine. Someone always had marijuana, so we would drink and smoke, then go back to class. At this school, there were some big-name girls and boys who got together for whatever.

Early in the year, I had hooked up with a dude who had a nice reputation, such as the one I boasted. We would go to school, then catch the bus downtown in time to catch the real high schoolers going to lunch. Here we are thinking we're cool running into Lazarus to spray cologne on then hit the corner to holler at the girls. Good girls do like bad boys.

My guy Nell wound up catching a robbery case and getting sent away for a year. This sent me running back with the super-wild bunch. Strange as it may seem, we were loyal to one another. But everyone has their limits. I thought we were supposed to be scared of nobody and have each other's back no matter what. Yet I felt like I didn't belong.

We were in the gym shooting basketball, and I guess the teacher had had enough of my mess. So he snatched me up real good. My dudes got him off me, but we didn't do to him what we had done to so many other people who crossed us. The strange thing is they went on to make fun of me for this grown man shaking a little kid up. These same dudes got caught stealing with me and told on me. The police told my mom when she picked me up that I had no business with these guys. I was the only one who wouldn't talk, and they were older than me.

In the process, I was stealing clothes, shoes, money, whatever. Whatever I could on a daily basis. Along with this, I was meeting girls who had heard about me. I took a couple girlfriends. My main squeeze at the time was the older cousin of a girl I used to talk to from time to time. She had one of them co-op jobs. It's like she goes to school for two weeks, then works for two weeks. This was big props to have a girl with a job by this time. By the end of the first quarter of school, I had managed to get kicked out of the alternative school. This was the last straw.

The board of education was trying to tell my mom I couldn't go to school at all. My mom wasn't having me sitting in her house all day, legit like that, so she raised a little fuss. We had a meeting downtown at the board of education to discuss my dilemma. This was at the same time we discovered there was another Horace James Gullatte III. My father had neglected to tell us he had another son named after him. When this was discovered I was in a meeting about my involvement as one of the leaders of the Young Dogs. I was placed on some kind of school probation.

The man I was supposed to report to, I only saw him once at that meeting. Anyway, at the meeting of the education board, they allowed me to go to any school I wanted to go to. The school in my district was very adamant about not having me back. I chose Fairview because my cousin went there. Going to this school was sweet because all the kids lived in the middle class. They dressed nice and always had money. There were only about three bad boys in the whole school.

With my reputation and my cousin's rep, things were pretty nice. The principal was a man I had known. He sat me down the first day and gave me his rules. All he said was, "This ain't Roth Intermediate and don't have your boys coming up here after school." Oh yeah, and the famous, "I ain't having it here." There was a rule—no sweat suits worn to school. They would allow me to wear my sweat suits with an agreement that I wouldn't cause any trouble.

Meanwhile, every day after school my dudes would be outside waiting for me. Usually they had a stolen car or were trying to fight somebody or coming to see the ladies. This is about the time I got my first taste of lockup. Me, Bruce and Evan got caught stealing again and wound up in juvenile detention for two weeks. I got an extra five days for being a follower. When I got back to school, things were even better. My cousin had started giving me joints to take to school to sell for him. So before class, I got a couple dudes, and we would go smoke one.

One particular day, I got this little dude who I thought was pretty cool. He was a little crazy, plus he liked the ladies. We smoked a joint. Later that day, his mom had to come and get him. He started tripping too hard. This was the last time I saw my man. I heard his mom and dad placed him in a job corp.

In total, I may have lasted one month at this school without counting the nineteen days of jail. The reason for this is because a small riot broke out and a few people got beat up. This was on a Friday, so things got really out of hand. Monday back at school, I'm late as usual, but this time it's an all-points bulletin for me on site. I got to class and was sent straight to the principal's office. He blamed me for the whole thing. I can't believe they told on me.

The principal yelled at me something serious, got on the phone, and called my old school. I was given forty-five minutes to get from one principal's office to the next. Bottom line, when school started, I was at Fairview Intermediate, and at the end of the day, I came out of Roth Intermediate. Being back around the guys I grew up with wasn't all that bad. The only thing was most of my classmates were younger than me because of my failing the ninth grade the first time.

A guy named Wendall became my every-day running buddy. We both had ties to the neighborhood and the gang. At this time, we were seeking more knowledge of the game. A couple of older cats taught us how to do a three-car molly and hide the ball with the three caps. Wendell was the pretty-boy type. So we did a lot of gaming on the ladies. You could say Wendell and I became real tight, because we would buy or steal the same clothes or dress alike. This could have been another situation where I didn't fit in because a lot of times things would get awkward.

I'm no longer playing sports or even thinking about them. My dream to play center field for the Cincinnati Reds has long been gone and replaced with a false illusion of becoming a hustler. Wendell and I would exchange girlfriends, hustle other dudes, and steal whenever given the chance. We both had grown accustomed to having $20 to $30 in our pockets at all times. We would rock forty ones with a $10 or $20 wrapped around them, trying to make our knots seem bigger than what they were.

Downtown was the place to hang out. So every day we would catch the bus downtown and hang out with all the other troubled kids. This is where the conversation was struck up about who had been sent away to do time in a boys' school. Everyone in this conversation, which was ten to fifteen deep, had been sent away but me. The joke became that Horace was still in the minor leagues because he hadn't been sent away. I decided in order to get my street cred, I had to get sent away. Wendell and I did our thing for a while, but there were always some jealous or envious dudes. And the ones seeking some revenge.

One particular day downtown hanging, this older dude had a beef with Wendell over some girl. He ran up on Wendell talking, and they began fighting. Wendell ended up getting out on him but ran after the fight broke up. The dudes were getting on him for trying to jump on the young guy, and since he had lost and Wendell pulled out, dude wanted to fight me.

One of my best friends named Bryant, his cousin Marsha, a friend of mine was in between me and the dude with his boys holding him back. Marsha tells me that it ain't worth it, plus Wendell left you. So I got on the bus with Marsha looking at Wendell across the street. I felt bad for leaving Wendell like that, but yet another situation that tells me I'm out of my league.

After getting home chilling, here comes Wendell and the crew talking about jumping on me because I left him. Needless to say, I didn't go outside. But the beef went on for some time without us ever really getting into it, mainly due to my avoiding him the majority of the time.

Because the hood had flipped on me to a degree, I had the ones riding with me and the ones riding with him. At any event, my quest to make a name for myself was still on. For the majority of the summer, I spent making moves and pumping weights, waiting on the day Wendell and I would run into each other. The new school year was about to start, and I wasn't really feeling like going back to school. The first few days were OK, but I had other plans. Hanging out with a friend of mine riding around, we stopped at a car lot and were just checking out some cars. When I got inside one to look from the driver's seat, the keys were right there in the ignition. So I grabbed the keys to a black Trans Am with a T-Top. So I could have someone to roll with me, I grabbed another set of keys on my way out of the lot.

Getting back to the house, I called my main man Lamar. Me and Lamar are like best friends. Our mothers were best friends coming up, plus we grew up on the same block. Now really it's three of us who ran in the big wheel days and still kick it. Lamar is also the buddy who wanted to trade girlfriends with me and somehow put the trick down on me to get both of the girls.

After telling him my plan, we both agreed that I would walk to his house, and then when it became late enough, we would walk to the car lot, leaving the only way back by foot or by wheels. On the way to the car lot, we looked for thirty-day temps to steal and put on the stolen cars. As we got close to the lot, my adrenaline was pumping hard. Nervousness was in the air also. The lights on the car lot were bright, as to show off the cars at night. We made our move, ducked down to put the tags on, then hit it. We came off the lot rolling.

Having that car for two weeks was the most exciting period of my short life. I was riding around talking about my father's car, not going to my school, but at every other school. Meeting females and having fun with it. Lamar and I hooked up a lot, but we still did our own thing.

My boy Nell had just come home from boy's school after doing that year. So we started riding around. We hooked up with some girls from the other side of town. These were the girls the big boys were dating. The car was getting young Horace all the props he could handle. The girl who chose me was a twin, so you know I'm talking fly. Initially, we were supposed to take the cars to the chop shop and sell them for $300. Even though they were getting out on us because we were young, $300 was still a lot of money for a sixteen-year-old in 1986.

I went to this shop several times, but never could get out of the car. The police ended up snatching Lamar's car in his hood, and a fellow Young Dog who was on probation with me and Lamar told our PO that we were stealing cars. By me being already on the run for an assault, I had a don't-care attitude. The assault case stemmed from a gang fight where an innocent dude got his jaw broken, and of course, they blamed me. My aunt Trudy worked at the juvenile detention center, so some of her friends showed me favor, but this was it.

Because of that, things only got worse. I came up with a plan to break into an outlet store but needed some help to get it done. My partners Lamar; Nell, who just got out from doing a year; and Deke, who was on the run from a group home, and I got together to make the plan to fit everyone. Then we waited. This was a Friday night, and the football games were jumping. While the fellows went to the game, I spent time with the twin. This would be the first time we had sex, and unfortunately the last time we would see each other for a while.

The outlet store was out where the police were kind of partial toward black teens in a car. Before attempting the break-in, we got swooped by the police, and the moment of truth came. My fellows were already like, "I can't go back to jail," so I gave them the pass to tell the police it was my father's car. Sitting in the police car, I took the blame and let my dudes go. The police made them walk home and took me to jail.

Another Level

This time it wasn't no calling my mom, and she was not coming to get me. Straight to the DH, the detention home. From previous stays, I know to crack for the brand -new gym shoes, jeans, underclothes, and T-shirts. It never dawned on me what was happening until thirty days later I'm lying in the back of a station wagon headed up the highway to reformatory school. Six months to plead out to grand theft and the assault case goes away.

My first day sitting in the reception area, here comes Law J and Mike D. They were my home boys from the hood. After two weeks of orientation, when they decided your aggressive level, then placed you accordingly, my group was five six. This was a group of semi-aggressive dudes who clowned all day. My stay on five six was only until my first evaluation. Then I was moved to five four, the most aggressive group in the camp. Five Four Dogs was the moniker, and the staff fit the bill. With a mixture of guys from Dayton, Columbus, and Cincinnati, all the other cities south of Ohio, earning stripes was the order. On five four there were only three white guys in the beginning. Two of them would fight anyone and could win. The other one had to leave this group because of malnutrition. Every day there was a fight or two. I had my run-ins with dudes, won some fights, and continued to hustle. You could buy cigarettes from the staff and resell to the other inmates for a higher price. One forty-ounce beer cost $5, and joints were two for $10. I ended up in a big fight that landed me and a few more of us in Columbus Juvenile Center for aggravated inciting a riot. In the end, we all wound up doing dead time, which is time that doesn't count toward our sentence.

The whole time I was in Buckeye Youth Camp, my mom came to see me every week to show her support for her son. It was at Buckeye that I discovered my love for lifting weights. Even though in the past I had lifted and worked out some, I made the weight-lifting team here and chose it over the travel basketball team.

Every weekend, we could use the phone. I would call my cousin and kick it with him. Also while I was gone, crack cocaine became a big hit. Lamar had been sending me pictures of him at clubs with a bunch of money. Everybody was dressed and had cash. My cousin and his crew had made a move on this also. When calling my cousin, we would call girls on the three-way, you know, stuff like that. Twin had written to me for a couple months, but that stopped. My cousin informed me that she was smoking crack, so that really left several other girls for me to talk to. One was writing and accepting my calls but dating my cousin.

Boys' school was a learning experience and also a respect builder. There I was, back on the streets after doing my time, and faced with the same situation I had before going away. My mom wanted to treat me like a little boy, and I wanted to be a man. I was seventeen and thought I was ready to step up to the plate.

Being home two weeks, the outlet store that had eluded me before my capture was in my sights. This time with a successful attempt. My first days were more than I had expected. As soon as we arrived at the house, my cousin pulled up in this new Cadillac Deville. It was a change, because before I had left to do the seven months, everybody was walking. He rode me around filling me in on the latest events, showing me what's the haps. We had some drinks, smoked some weed.

Everything was going well until we went to pick up his girl from school. When she saw me, she started screaming. This was the one who was writing and accepting my calls while I was gone away. Now my cousin got mad and took me home, and out the window goes our relationship. We never were close after that point.

While sitting in the house, relaxing, talking to my mom, my brother called and told me to meet him over at my stepmom's house. When I got over there, my brother Dale had brought Twin over there to see me. Somehow they met through a mutual friend. So Twin and I picked up where we left off before I was sent away.

At this time, my running partner was a dude by the name of Head. This dude was pretty scandalous. Before I went away, we had hooked up a few times and had some fun, so now it was on. He had access to a car, and we were off to the races.

My thing was to break into the game. All my boys were getting down, and the money looked nice. Lamar gave me my first shot at the game. He pushed me $50 to buy a double up. I went to the block. These didn't exist before I left. Now folks are standing out on corners and running up on cars selling dope. Every project in the city, literally hundreds of dudes, women, kids hanging out on one street fighting to get a dollar. I'm not from the projects, but a residential area. Don't confuse residential from the suburbs, because West Wood ain't the suburbs. Anyhow, I rode up and gave it a shot.

My first attempt, I got played by some dude named Fast Black. Why would anybody buy dope from a dude named Fast Black? The corner wasn't my style. Not in somebody else's hood, anyway. In the meantime, my brother was onto something, but he was trying to do it with outsiders instead of his family. So that made me mad. Plus, he was allowing some chick to dictate whether I could drive his car or what he can do for me. Since he was tripping like that, I stole his necklace and sold it to have money to go to a concert with my girl.

My girl at the time was this girl named Gina. We had met when we were fourteen and fifteen years old. We stayed in touch, and when I went away, she rode the wave with me. Her family lived in the suburbs and had decent money for a black family. Between running the streets trying to come up with Head, Gina had become my heart. She was actually good for me, but we were too much alike. We both were Capricorns with our birthdays two days apart. Gina was also fine with a lot of body on a small waist. It was the beginning of the summer when I got out of the youth camp, so things between us got heated up quick.

Head and I were on some sleazy stuff. We were stealing, robbing, scheming every chance we could get, just to make a buck.

Because of my down-for-whatever attitude, a few good opportunities came our way. Sitting in the house waiting on Head, a dude named slick came by telling me there was an old man with a bank book loaded with money around the corner. So here I go off to hit the lick. The old man had $1,500 in his pocket. Head and I hung out with Slick for a couple days. Within these couple days, I jumped on my girl because she was worried about me, telling me these two dudes I'm with ain't my friends.

We also got involved with smoking primos, cocaine-laced weed joints. We also picked up a girlfriend of mine and her buddy. I had to stop these two from raping my girl's buddy. They were literally on top, about to make it happen.

The summer finally ended with a lot of drama. My brother was looking for me, and a bunch of bad blood between me and a bunch of people. I decided to go back to school and give it an honest try.

While in boys' school, my grades were good, and I actually learned something. MeadowDale was the high school of choice. One of my best friends was going there, so we went there together. The principal of MeadowDale was my old probation officer that I had a few years back from the gang involvement. He remembered me. So of course here goes another speech. Everything was going smooth. I'm attending school, not hanging out much, but getting it done. Then here comes the knock on my back door. The way the knock sounded, because don't nobody came to the back, I knew it was something. I got to the door, and it was some partners outside needing my assistance. In the end, I ended up involved in a kidnap/robbery turned murder for a lousy thousand dollars, and evidence in my mother's house.

I should have known better than to mess with these dudes, because in the summer, they had me tied up in another robbery turned into a brawl at the LL Cool J concert. Yet another example that I didn't belong in the game. My loyalty and dedication often led me to being used, and not understanding the cutthroat business we lived in, I just became a part of it.

From the proceeds of this debacle, I started another drug enterprise that lasted just a little longer than the previous ones. Eventually, school became just school. And in the end, I got thrown out again. My attention was focused on getting me some money. Also, my girl Gina decided she wanted to move on. This hurt because she was my first love. I never really got over her; my love for her just kept getting transferred from female to female. So now, the quest to obtain a kilo of cocaine was my main focus.

Dope Man

So school was no longer on my to do list. Head and I were full-time hanging again, this time with the intent to become dope boys. Because I didn't have any money to buy the dope, the higher up boys instituted a program called The Front. A guy I had known from the streets fronted me a five-pack, which cost $500. Because Head and I were together, we split it with my name being accountable for the payback.

It actually was doing pretty good advancing to a thousand-dollar package, but then we got slick, decided to make another move with my man's money choosing to get back with him later. We made the move, and it went well. But, as it goes things didn't go as planned. My man was looking for me for his money. I would see him, hit him with a story, and give him a hundred at a time, stuff like that. After messing that money up, I needed to get back on my feet. Things between Head and I were getting strained because we didn't really share the same view about hustling. My sister's boyfriend from Detroit had drug houses around Dayton, so he took me down to one of his spots and let me do some work with some of his Detroit homeboys. All this was taking place just before my eighteenth birthday. Somewhere I heard on your eighteenth birthday you were supposed to drink until you threw up. So that's just what happened to me. Me and the boys, Head and Bryant, we drank a case of Michelob Ultra.

The first night in the dope house probably changed my life, or at least altered it. This is where I finally learned how to sell dope. At this point, I'd given a woman some crack for sex, but obviously

I was so sweet, because my first personal favor in the dope house, the crew seen what I gave the chick and let me have it.

Now, I see how come I was a favorite. The first night I made something like $300 or something close. This was only maybe from 8:00 that night to the morning. Being excited about this event, I ran up to Lamar's house and told him about it. I had no idea about staying in the dope house for days straight, but Lamar informed me about how things worked, so eventually I got the hang of selling dope and making money.

My wardrobe started to get bigger, dope fiends bringing all kinds of appliances, clothes, jewelry, etc through the house. My first car was a '74 Lincoln Town Car, powder blue with a crushed velvet interior. By this time, the weather had started breaking back warm, and instead of me sitting in the house I was responsible for drop-offs and pickups, plus I would find houses and put people in them. This would later become a mistake because I would get guys who I grew up with but wasn't as ready or down enough to keep it real, so I had guys running off with thousand dollar packs. Plus, I was getting my grind off, so sometimes it would be my money. The sad part was it was like a chain of command. The higher up you were, the less work you had to do, but the more money you would handle.

With the more money people were handling, the more money they were stealing. During this moment of my life, the girl who replaced Gina was Charlotte. I met her at the disco, and she was cool. I can't say I really liked her, but she was cool and available. Also within this mix was a couple girls, three sisters and a friend. Charlotte was the younger sister of Duke, who I helped get down with some money, and he was going with one of the sisters.

Gene was another guy who was down with us, and he had their friend. Lamar ended up getting down also, and he had a sister. I wound up with the big sister. All the girls including Charlotte went to the same school, so this was always a mess. Charlotte ended up sleeping with Gene, and then his girl and I ended up sleeping together for revenge, and then we also became really, really close. Gene was pretty slick with ladies, so it didn't matter to him, but he spent a big portion of his time trying to get back at me.

After some time went by, the Detroit boys had trouble keeping workers in the spots. They started depending on me a lot to keep the spots with people and the money coming. They would say the reason to bring down dudes from their city to Dayton was because they didn't know their way around, so they wouldn't be trying to kick it but would stay in the spots and hustle. Like all things, it's the good, the bad, and here comes the ugly.

The first sign of things to come was a bad batch of boys from Detroit. These boys liked to get high, and some even smoked the pipe. Since I was in charge of keeping things together, I spent most of the time with them and their bad habits. We would smoke weed laced with crack, calling them primos together. The bigger problem was these boys were in the spot that made the most money.

Gene, Duke, and Lamar were in a new spot we had just turned out. The money spot had started getting slow because competition started getting larger in the area. Then the crew from Detroit ran off with dope and money. It was a scramble for me to place dudes in the dope house who weren't scared because the police were coming around a lot, and the beef with the guys who were short stopping customers before they could get to the door was getting deeper.

In the meantime, Gene, Duke, Lamar, we are doing our thing. We're receiving a lot of love from the streets because we were getting money. Before us hooking up, Gene and Lamar already had things going on, so us coming together only made better music. Myself, my game had elevated to gold rings on every finger, diamond-cut chains with my initials HG on them.

I had a Wittnauer four-diamond watch, silk outfits with snakeskin belts, all the hundred-dollar gym shoes and $500 glasses, plus I could boast a bankroll of $3,000. At this point in my life, this was lovely, 1988, the beginning of something serious. Lamar and Gene had a partner of theirs who evidently had a problem with them. There was beef about a couple hundred dollars, so Dirty decided to burn Gene's car up fresh out the shop. Gene shoots up Dirty's car, and now it's drama. I had nothing to do with this, but we are all still doing our thing. We were coming from eating out in two separate cars. Duke was in the front by himself with Lamar, Gene and myself behind in my car. Dirty doesn't see us, but catches Duke and rides on him hard, shooting at him.

By the time we caught up, Dirty wanted to talk, but Lamar started shooting at Dirty. We pull up to Gene's house, get out of the car while Gene goes in the house to reload, Dirty was riding with his girl while she was driving, and he was sitting on the window seal shooting over the roof. Folks were scrambling like crazy. Me, I was just standing there tripping. Then Dirty started shooting at me, and now it's something.

I grabbed the gun from Gene, who was shaking like crazy, and ran out in the yard, and unloaded the gun at Dirty. Thanks be to God that no one got hit. We became the talk of the town, and also my first shootout. No sooner after this shootout, Gene, Lamar, and Duke ran off with the money. I don't really care. It wasn't my money. The fact that they played me after needing help getting on their feet is the only problem I had. Dirty, Gene, and Lamar end up making things right with each other, but this was the beginning of bad blood between me and Dirty. A lot of things were changing within the Detroit crew. They started really pushing me to handle everything, because they wanted to go party. Now instead of giving me the pack to drop off and bring the money right back, I was receiving $10,000 packages and bringing all the money at once.

The pay went like a job. These guys paid $500 a week and runners a thousand. My hustle came by taking all $10,000 worth of rocks and chopping a piece off each one of them. Then I would bag them up and send them to the houses as packages. Somehow the money started getting real funny because dudes coming up with new cars and everything.

This was the first time I had met the head man himself. He came to check out what was happening. Since my sister has a baby by one of them, the meeting place would sometimes be over at my mom's. This particular time, there was no one to blame but me and my two recruits for the losses. So here we are being questioned by six dudes over 200 pounds apiece about some money we couldn't possibly have had anything to do with. The only thing is I'm little junior. Can't do nothing to me, so they were harder on my guys than they were on me.

After they hit my dudes Head and Bryant with skillets and threw around threats, they went outside to talk. This was the moment I knew I was crazy because I had this rage to shoot all of them with the Uzi I stole from them. The one thing that got me under control was I had been stealing from them and was sitting real nice. While they hung out laughing at us, I was sitting back laughing at them, thinking about all the dope and the money that they didn't find while they were running through my mom's house. And the bankroll that I was hiding was in my mom's closet, some place that they wouldn't disrespect.

So then they made me get in the car and show them where Gene, Lamar, and Duke stayed. We rode around for a little bit with me not really knowing where they stayed, and they started giving me the speech about being down and being loyal, you know, this and that. But by the end, I was still needed because I was the only real link between them and Dayton. So I got put back on house duty for a week or so, and then one Friday, all the Detroit boys were going back home for another activity. There was only a small amount of dope left, so we cooked it all up and came up with a hundred-dollar block. To this point, all that was being served was $50 double ups.

After making the first few, I was asked my opinion, because this was something nobody had done. I was like roll with it. I was given $24,000 worth of hundred-dollar blocks to go down to the hottest spot we had. Everybody was coming back on Monday, so this gave me the weekend to get it done. The spot usually yielded between $10 to $12,000 a day. I went and got Bryant and Head, and we went to the spot, and like gangbusters we sold $24,000 worth of rocks in two hours. The hustle boys got word of the hundred-dollar blocks and was buying them ten at a time. My crew and I made every one of the overs. We got away with some great pocket change. This would be the last real successful day in this spot because it got raided with nobody home.

Holding My Own

With the money-making spot down, there was a scramble to replace it. We were still working out of two spots, but the money wasn't coming in so good. Someone found a spot in the projects. I was asked to start the spot up with one of their boys. This spot didn't feel right at all, plus this dude loved the crack and the women too much. The house owner was some crazy dude whose claim to fame was knowing karate real good and beating up a bunch of Secret Service men.

I stayed two days tops in this mess and pulled out. I'm glad I did because the crazy guy wound up killing their boy a couple days later. So now my new spot is in Trenton. Trenton is this little place located on the outside of Westwood, the hood I grew up in. So I was responsible for running the Trenton spot and keeping up with other spots as well. By this time, I had tore up the Lincoln, left it with the bumper hanging off, and I tore up my new station wagon. The new car I bought was a '77 Camaro, which was in the shop getting painted and hooked up.

The spot on Trenton is where my second oldest child was created. A boy, Jamie. His mom was someone from my neighborhood who wouldn't give me a shot growing up. Besides her being like a year older than me, she was super fly, and all the older guys were at her. We hooked up one time at the spot. The Detroit boys have been somewhat hit and miss around this time, and I was buying my own dope to keep the spot going.

I worked this spot until it couldn't be worked anymore, and like the other ones, this one would also get shut down. By this time, my car was ready; the Camaro hit the streets hard. Fire engine red with black stripes, spoiler kit, sitting on low-profile Michelins and three stars.

This was the time I started out on my own, not hanging out with anybody, because all my guys had played me about some money. My girl Charlotte was still around, but things were shaky between us. On top of everything else, I'd been in a relationship with one of my best friend's moms for almost a year now. I ran into a guy from my hood. We got to talking and discovered we both had like the same amount of money plus ambitions. We started going to King's Island and hanging out regularly until we started hustling together. Because neither of us was a true corner hustler, we had to find workers who were.

There were times we used the same workers, giving them $250 packs a piece. Some of the dudes under me from my hood was interested in getting down, so I turned them out to hustling. Vincent, Cole, and Rich were some true hustlers. I would let them drive my car, or we would hang out in the hood together. We did a lot of things like that, even though my guy Tricky and I hustled together didn't mean we spent our money in the same places. Our connections were different. His turned out to be more reliable than mine.

Wendell was my current connection. I felt I couldn't grow with him. Tricky kept telling me to roll with his guy, but I was loyal. Wendell's cousin was dating Rachel, my son's mother, before he got sent away to a youth camp. Her and I met while he was gone, and now he is out. She is pregnant, and they try to make a big deal out of this. Without me knowing she's pregnant by me, because we hadn't talked since the night she pulled a knife on me. All the conversations were saying that the baby wasn't mine. I never needed any convincing because we only had sex once.

Things got bad between Wendell and me once again because I owed him some money, which I didn't have. On top of this one, I had gotten jumped and robbed for my jewelry in Cincinnati at a concert by some guys older than me, while the other five guys I was with just watched.

I was sitting at home feeling depressed because my money was low, my jewelry gone. I owe one guy and beefing with a family of brothers for robbing me. Tricky came by to get me to kick it. We were riding, and we saw one of the brothers who jumped on me. Tricky tells me the brother wants to talk to me. I wanted to holler at him too. We pulled over to the left to holler. He straight up told me he doesn't have no beef with me, but his brothers do. He pointed across the street, and here came two on a motorcycle and a Blazer full of dudes. One brother on the bike had a two-by-four and swung it freely. Tricky tried to do what he could. In the end it was too many. I had to run to get away. They wouldn't mess with Tricky because of his family, but I was fair game.

After getting away, I ran to this girl's house. I called to the hood, over to my guys' house where our friends would usually hang out at. These guys didn't run the streets but were all big guys. My man Mike came to pick me up and tell me, "We're all over Curt's house hanging out." I had Mike ride down the strip trying to track these dudes down. We didn't see them on Gettysburg but found them riding down my street looking for me back in the hood.

I had Mike stop, and I got up in the truck to tell them to follow us around the corner. They followed us to my guy Curt's house. Immediately, the fellows stood up, and one of my Young Dogs' homies Leslie was over there. At the sight of this, the guys who wanted to hurt me earlier started not being so aggressive. The lead guy, the one who slammed me, punched me in the mouth, hit me with the two by four. Now, he is saying he heard I was going to shoot his mother's house up with my uzzi. Leslie and I were screaming for some work, but in the end, Curt's mom came out and made them go away, and me also. After this occasion, my guy Leslie and I started running real tight, tighter than bros.

My brother Daniel hooked me up with this older chick named Rochelle who used to mess with Leslie's brother, but it didn't matter because Rochelle was just someone I messed with.

Because of my money status, there wasn't a whole lot going on. Now, I'm flat broke and in debt. Rochelle gave me a few hundred here and there, but my luck won't break. Plus, I had to spend the night with her and go through the motions to get the money. Again, while I was chilling at the house, Tricky came by with a guy we grew up with. Tricky was telling him about my circumstances, so dude came offering some work. I took it because, hey, I'm down on my luck.

This venture started out going well. The first time I got an ounce, then it continued up to two at a time. Wendell got word of me doing some things and came for his money. I was down $3,000 to Wendell, so you know he is trying to collect. One night, Wendell caught me riding, and he and another guy strong-armed me out of my new connect's money. Now I owe Wendell a thousand, and my new connection $2,000.

My new connect didn't like the situation one bit. He wanted his money from me, but he really had a problem with Wendell anyway, because of their already existing beef. So it had escalated for them. Within two weeks of this fallout, my car got set on fire in front of my mom's house, so now there's no car, and I owe not one, but two dudes who want their money.

In the meantime, Leslie and I were still hanging out tough. I'm trying to figure out a way to get some money. Then here comes the Detroit boys back in town needing a place to make it happen. This was an opportune time for me because I was flat broke. We found a spot back in the project which was where their boy had gotten killed. Leslie came with me to help get the spot off the ground. Things are always slow starting a new spot, but it picked up. I would see Wendell from time to time to give him a hundred here and there. I wasn't thinking about the other guy too deep because they burned my car up.

One of Leslie and mines favorite places to eat out was Cassano's Pizza. There were only two you could sit down at during this time, so when we would be out of dope and just hanging out, we would go out to get something to eat in the suburbs. As a joke, we asked the manager for a job. We filled the applications out and got hired on the spot. Leslie's first day was my third day and both of our last day.

With the hustle, things were better than they had been. Leslie and I started putting the force into the game. Having two riot pumps in the spot and a baseball bat with us at all times, we were about letting these fools have it, jumping out swinging that ball bat was our favorite.

Staying in the spot for days on end, leaving only to make food and drink runs. After one of those weeks straight without a bath, hair cut, or change of clothes. It was my turn to make the food run.

I'm in line at Kentucky Fried Chicken not really paying any attention. My head was down when I stepped up to the counter, the voice said to me, "Welcome to Kentucky Fried Chicken. May I help you?" I started giving my order, and all I see is the prettiest hands I've ever seen tapping on the cash register. Then the voice started registering in my head. When I looked up, I knew right there I had to have her. From this point I started popping my game. Come to find out, her name was April, and she had already heard about Horace Gullatte.

I left with the food charged, but didn't ask for her number. Driving back to the spot like Batman. Leslie sat there smirking at me as I told him about the chick I met, and how I'm going to have her. The reason for his smirking was because my woman, Rochelle, was still around and a couple more, but Lyndsey had become queen bee in my life, and I had it bad for Lyndsey.

Lyndsey was one of the slickest females I have ever messed with at the time. When I say this, she knows how to play the game, and how to use her body, which she did a lot of. The next day I went and got a haircut, took a bath, got fresh, ready to pull up on this April girl. I had replaced my jewelry from the robbery with a couple rings, a watch, and a cable rope with an emblem. I've always loved sweat suits, so I have one of them on ready to come up.

Going into Kentucky Fried, feeling confident. On site April knew what I was there for. We arranged for me to pick her up after work and take her home. Picking her up, she comes out with her friend asking me to give her a ride. This friend had been a friend to a couple of my friends, so I didn't really care for her, but because of my goal to put this honey in the car, got to roll with it. Arriving at the friend's house, April asked could she run in real quick leaving her purse in the car. The chick left me outside for twenty minutes like a sucker. I pulled out on her. We eventually hooked back up because I really wanted her now.

She became very special to me for many reasons. The main character trait which attracted me was first she was easy to talk to, and second, it took me a month to have sex with her the first time, and another month to get it again. I was only waiting a week at this time for anybody, or I pulled out. Meanwhile, my hustle was still thriving, and Leslie also was getting his end. Like always, there's some bad coming. The start of the bad came like a bad dream this time.

First, I'm in the hood grabbing some wings at the chicken place when Wendell and his two cousins pulled up on me about $200. The word on the street is that I'm getting money again, plus jumping out of rental car after rental car, and popping out at the club, Superfresh, the dude thought I was playing him, which for real I was. I never forgot when you put it down on me, player.

The dude jumps in the car and asks me for his money, nicely. I told him, "Let's go around to my house," so I can give him his money. While coming through the alley, he started popping this gangster *Scarface* garbage to me. I had enough of this dude, so I pulled my gangster out on him. My exact words were, "You want to shoot something? I'm going to show you how to shoot something." Now I'm speeding to get to the house to get this chump what he was looking for. My mom heard me screeching up and ran outside. She had taken my gun from me, because she had found it in her house, so I'm jumping out yelling, "Go get my gun for me. I'm going to show this dude how to start shooting somebody."

He was stuck, he wasn't ready for that. Now him and his cousins looking stupid while I paraded through them letting them know they weak. My mom ain't for the gun play, so she tells me and Wendell to take it around the corner one-on-one to settle this shit. Pulling around the alley, we both got out of the car and threw up our hands only to dance around and not do nothing. Because of his attitude, instead of giving him the whole $200, he received $100 and, "I'll see you later."

The Detroit boys had been out of town for a couple weeks, so Leslie and I were buying our own pack and selling it out the spot. The same guy who had control over the money before was still in control. Same old story. Money got messed up. And this time, I looked really guilty. This time, I was. I was getting mine mainly because of me being Little Junior. Once again, they rolled down on me, throwing threats, taking my bat, smashing stuff with it, and taking the dope off the plate we had. Oh yeah, we got put out of the spot also. So we went shopping, getting prepared for the New Year, '89 style.

Celebrating New Year's at Club Spunky's with bottles of Dom Perignon. Sitting in the booth across the club, I spot three females coming in the door. My sister worked at the club, so I had her invite the girls over to drink Dom P with us. Three came, but only two stayed. The one who left was the one I wanted, but she had a man already there, so we tossed up a few, danced a lot, and by the end of the night we were at breakfast, then a hotel. I still can't remember the girl I was with because after dropping them off, I didn't ask for her number or nothing. Since that night, I saw her maybe five times in the year to come.

Losing the spot left no place to sell dope and stopped me from making free money. Once again, I'm down on my luck and scrambling with some change. Leslie is still my main friend, but there were things I had to do, like hooking back up with Head and a guy named Dwight. I've known Dwight all my life. His older sister was my godmother. He has two kids with my best friend Bryant's mom, and my brother had a baby with his little sister.

By this time Head had developed a serious primo problem. I would still smoke one every now and then, maybe two. Dwight was fresh off hitting the pipe but still liked primos. So here we are, three brothers trying to get some money and support a habit. As far as my love life, it was getting crazier by the minute. Lyndsey ended up pregnant, and it couldn't have been mine because we hadn't had sex. April and I went through some stuff, because she found out about the other women. Charlotte finally cut me all off. Rochelle was still around getting on my nerves. The end result was Rochelle was all I had left. Her and $75.

Teaming up with Dwight, he had $75, I had $75 and my brother Daniel had the dope. We took our $150 to Daniel to buy some dope because I knew he would make it right for his lil brother. So, we used my connection, Dwight had the customers. We set up shop at his sister's, my nephew's apartment all day, trying to turn this into a spot. All the sales mainly came off Dwight's beeper. The profit we were making we would split, and then we had another bankroll for re-up.

During these times, Rochelle and I had gotten close because she was the only one around. She stuck with me during this tough time and I played her for it, but only now in my later years do I thank her for it.

1989

Joy was my brother's baby mama, and Dwight's little sister. Because of us being around each other every day, all day, arguments would take place. In this small two-bedroom apartment a lot of things went down. Joy and Dwight's older sister were there with her two boys. Joy had two boys, and their nephew was living there with his girlfriend and her child. I became the man of the house. Everyone looked to me to handle everything, but it was cool.

My father had gotten remarried to this lady named Bobbi, and she had a daughter named Staci, who my father adopted. She used to be down to the apartment also. There were times that I had to discipline her, not by force or nothing, but by making her sit down because she was bad. Evidently my discipline didn't approve with her mom because she decided to check me, which was cool, but she had these long fingernails and poked me in the face. It took four people to restrain me from doing something to her. Later that evening, two things happened. First my father called over to the apartment, telling me he was going to kill me. And second, everyone left for some reason or another, and Joy and I discovered why we argued so much. We ended up in the bed.

All I had in my little safe at Rochelle's was $50, plus I had re-up money for a package, and also there was supposed to be another stash over at Dwight's house. My mom called me for $150 or something, so I called Dwight to get $100 of our money. This is when I discovered his wife and him were getting high on a whole different level, so I couldn't get my mom all she asked for, but it was time to make a move. All we were buying at the time was a quarter ounce, and this was being split between us. My brother had gotten tired of giving more than I paid for, so he cut me off. The guy we bought from now was from our hood. He was an older, successful dope dealer, but his prices were high. We would go to buy, and there would be a couple dudes over his house in the basement, shooting pool, snorting cocaine, smoking weed and drinking. After a couple purchases, I decided this would be the last time I buy from him, and the partnership between Dwight and I was over.

Getting back to the spot, I cooked up the dope like always in a baby bottle. Dwight and I went to the bathroom to cut the dope up. We cut up $500, a nice double-ups. This was where I made my move. I smacked the dope all over the bathroom, got up in his face and told him the partnership was over and this all my dope. Because he had been playing me anyway, he accepted it. Now, I have all the dope in the house, banging the person whose name was on the lease, and running the house. I had to get every bit of the $500 on this one. And I did it.

Through the grapevine, I heard about a dude selling ounces for $675. He was from my hood, so it wasn't hard to get in touch with him. The $675 was a little off, but $725 was the real price. He allowed me to owe him the $225. From this moment on, the spot started doing good. I was selling anywhere between $500 to $1,000 every day. Rochelle was right there bringing me food and brand-new jogging suits and shoes once or twice a week. I was sleeping two nights a week with Rochelle, the rest at the spot with Joy.

Joy didn't like Rochelle coming down, but I had no choice because she knew about Rochelle from the beginning. Plus, she got a baby with my brother. Another reason she didn't like Rochelle was because she knew my brother was still messing with Rochelle's sister. Just right when things started going good, my bankroll was maybe $1100 and rising, my car needed some brake work done. I just dropped it off and told them to fix it. When they called for me to come get it, the ticket was like $800 or $900. I can't remember exactly, but it was a chunk. I needed my car, but this would take all of my money.

I called Rochelle and told her. She told me to get my car, and Friday she would bring me enough money to buy an ounce. Leslie and I are still super tight, and like always with Leslie and me together, drama soon follows. Prior to me and Dwight posting up at Joy's, she had this boyfriend. I would always go down there to see my nephew and everyone else. I stepped in one night with Joy on the phone. Dude heard me talking and started checking Joy. I heard her explaining who I was and all that, so I got on the phone to talk to my mans. He started woofing, saying he's on his way. Me being myself I waited on the dude to get there.

He came with two other dudes. I met them outside and told them to do whatever they're going to do, because when the tables turned my way, me and my boys gone handle them. They let me go with talking junk. Some weeks go by, and I wasn't really thinking about them. One night, Leslie, Head, and I were going to see Joy, and the same dudes are leaving her apartment. This time it was my turn. We jumped on all of them. Chased those dudes down the street. Took the bat to their car windows.

Several months passed. We weren't thinking about these dudes. Leslie goes over to his cousin's house, to chill with his aunt and family. A knock at the door made Leslie's cousin run to the door, stepping outside. Leslie heard some voices and looked outside to his cousin holding back Joy's dude talking about he's going to kill somebody. All this time, Leslie's cousin had been dating the dude who was telling her he was going to do something to us, and she never told us.

Leslie calls me to come and get him, telling me what went down. We strapped up to go look for these dudes. Leaving his aunt's house, we see dude and his cousin coming our way, plus with another car load of people. We didn't know the other car was filled with the girls, one being his older cousin, Billy's girl driving his car while he was in jail. Doing a U-turn, we caught up with him. Leslie with the .38 and me with the shotgun.

As soon as the car stopped, Leslie jumped out, shooting. I had to place the car in park and jumped out only to see Leslie's cousin dive in front of the dude. I hollered for Leslie to see his cousin in the car, not before shooting a few times and catching the dude before he finally sees his cousin trying to protect the dude. We didn't know she was in the car until we jumped out. Now we are on the run. Police are swarming for us, me really, because the girls in the other car told the police I had done it.

The police were looking for me everywhere they could look. Going to my step mom house they told her I did the shooting, she told us to go on the run because they didn't have the facts straight. Leslie's father made him turn himself in and admit the shooting. Leslie was bonded out straight out, after a couple days. Back at the spot, beef was picking up. I started to move an ounce a day, sometimes an ounce and a half. When you're on the grind like this, there isn't any time to go to the club or be out in public. With the way things were going, I'm thinking about my coming-out party. I have pictured myself wearing an all black full length leather jacket with leather pants, matching sweater: so putting the jacket on layaway, paying on it slowly until the time was right, was the plan.

Mr. $725 and I were building a nice relationship, then one day I couldn't get a hold of him. After trying a few times, I had to make another hookup. Five thousand dollars was my goal before taking a weekend to celebrate and hit the town and show everybody how

I bounced back. My relationship with Joy started getting ugly. I had this mean streak in me where sometimes it was hard to control my actions. And my relationships have violence in them with me being the main culprit.

Just right when I reached the $5,000 Mitch, she hit me with, "I'm moving," and she already had it in place, plus I had gotten my coat out, rented a luxury car, and bought some bad dope. I was still stepping out though. The club is where everyone made their comeback story.Showing the streets that we are back. I was dressed to kill and making mouths drop, looking good. All my dudes in the streets, plus the ladies were giving me props. Standing at the doorway kicking noise. In comes a fellow dressed in all white, sharp as hell.

The two sharpest guys in the place, I was one of them, with Dirty being the other. After the weekend, I had to make a decision on what to do, so I had Rochelle come down and get an apartment in her name. By the time I got the apartment, got the phone, some furniture and some accessories, my bankroll was $1200 and coming off spending $3300 for the bad dope, which should have taken care of everything and left me with five grand still.

After all the moving and stuff was over with, now it was time to get some dope. My previous connection had sold me the bad dope, so I wasn't calling him back. Every other number I had wasn't calling me back. Then I remembered this guy from my hood had been sending me messages to holler at him. He was the friend of Mr. 725. I rode down to where they be at, to find out Mr. 725 was locked up, and he had what I needed, so I bought one from him. After talking for a minute about the hood or whatever, he informed me that he would front me whatever I bought.

April

During this time of trying to get back on my feet, my motivation came from the women who left me during my tough times. Every one of them seemed to have a guy in their face with more money, a better car and better outcomes. I hadn't spoken to Lyndsey, Gina, April, or Charlotte. The only one who was constantly on my mind was April.

I had vowed to go back and get her, once my mission was complete. Keeping it strong, not to bother April, or come before my time was right, was hard. One time, I broke down and went to see her. Pulling up at her apartment, I noticed a moving truck in front of their apartment with her and her family putting boxes in it. They looked to be moving. I just pulled off and let things be.

So during the coming-out party, one of my plans was to pull up at Kentucky Fried Chicken, dressed to impress. When I stepped in the place, all eyes were on me. All April could do was smile, because she knew I was looking good. All the other girls working with her felt me also.

I went straight up to her. I asked, "What time you getting off?" She told me her stepfather was picking her up. I told her, "Tell him I got this." All she could do was smile and nod.

Picking her up and driving her straight home is when my spill began. Flat out, there wasn't any choice for her. She was strictly at the mercy of a man who really wanted her, who truly cared for her. We kissed and hugged, until she broke all the way down, and said, "You my man."

The confidence of having April back in my life was all I needed. My focus and determination intensified. With a new connection and partner on my team, things were looking even better.

The first night of being in a new dope spot was even better than being in the old one. I stocked the fridge with Miller Genuine Draft, plugged in the Nintendo, and I opened up for business. By the morning time, the one ounce was gone. Because I already had a little more change, it didn't take but a couple hundred more to buy two.

The next morning, I went to meet up with my new connect, with two-ounce money, I left with four. It was like, the more dope I bought, the more dope I will sell. Dwight since the bathroom incident started working for me, holding down the spot with me. My goal for every ounce was to make a thousand, with Dwight getting everything over that. It was only taking a day, at most, to go back to re-up. Every trip, I would go up one more ounce higher than the last time.

April and I spent a lot of time together, either on the phone, or me stopping by to see her, while taking a break from hustling. She was starting to reap the benefits of having a man who was taking care of his business. The job at Kentucky Fried Chicken had to go, mainly because I wanted to control her. I didn't like for the phone to ring more than twice, or I thought she was doing something. Though let me call, and someone doesn't answer the phone, Chief? I'm on my way.

She consulted with me about everything going on, going across the street to the store, she would call me. Within a month's time, I had managed to work my way up to a kilo. I also had that little safe at Rochelle's bulging with money. Because I had a strategy, the only money which got counted was the money I owed to my connect and how much money I needed to re-up for my own purposes. Everything else got thrown into the safe, uncounted.

Also, within this month's time, I bought a 77 green Ninety Eight Oldsmobile, and put some music in it, plus the Trues and Vogues. I was still renting the Cadillac for $450 a week.

Leslie, in the meantime, had his own spot, back down in Summer Courts, the same one the Detroit Boys had. Leslie really didn't like selling dope. Plus, he was out on bond from the shooting case. So everything was really just having fun for him. I would give him the dope for his spot. If he felt like paying for it, he did. If he didn't, he didn't. This was my best friend, and whatever, for him.

Even with the money flowing, the girls jumping, and April having my back, drama was my life. Leslie and I had this thing to go out to the shopping malls and play too much. Our main thing was to go to the toy section and slam the basketballs in the low rims. While doing this, I would be Magic, and he would be Jordan. Plus, we would check each other.

Doing this got us in trouble, because I slammed the ball, fell into two rows of toys, knocking them to the floor. Made a loud noise on top of us. We laughed out loud. We left the mess there and went over to the bikes and rode through the stores. All this, with three grand in my pocket, and Leslie with money, as well. The security called the police, and both of us got taken to jail. The more money I made, the bigger my head got.

At the spot, all kinds of things were going down. So many sex parties to the extent they got on my nerves sometimes. Every female who came through the door wanted to go to bed with me. Their reason was for me to be a little generous with my money, or my dope. My reputation was growing, so to the point of preparing the dope, dudes would leave their money, like a layaway. Literally, there would be two ounces or better sold on layaway before the dope was even ready.

April and I had a sex life, but it was not like some other relationships. April was special. She wasn't fast, trying to jump in the car to be seen with me. She never asked for money, and she was always easy to talk to or to laugh with. She would demand my time, Not, "Let's go to the movies," or stuff like that. We could sit on the couch and just have fun. Because she was my woman, I treated her to clothes, jewelry, etc. She always would go to the hairdresser every week, sometimes twice, if she wanted to. Leslie and April were super tight also. They had just as much fun together as Leslie and I had when she was around.

Life was really good for me. Reaching the first kilo was monumental, because this is all I wanted to be able to say that I had done. The first very kilo was sold, all rocks, ounce by ounce, rock by rock. The area had started banging so hard that two other guys got a spot in the same building. I was able to sell at the height of the spot, something like twelve ounces a day, with one guy doing six, and the other guy doing three.

Right after selling the first kilo, the landlord came to me and gave me a jump start to pull out, because the police were coming. So we packed it all in and moved to Summer Courts.

After the completion of that first kilo, Dwight and I went up to Rochelle's, to get the money right. I still hadn't counted all the money in the safe. Sitting in a room, Rochelle, Dwight and I started counting out the money, thousand-dollar stacks at a time. After counting my connect's money, it was time to count mines.

Getting through, I had my first $40,000. Dwight and Rochelle were just as happy as I was, because these two had helped me get there. I bagged the money up to take it for safer keepings. But before leaving, I hit Rochelle over the head with the statement, "You ain't never been hit with forty grand, ho."

April is originally from Kansas. Her father still lives there, with his wife and kids. April's younger sister had passed away. So she was going to Kansas for the funeral. Her bus was leaving at five in the morning, and she wanted me to be there, to see her off.

Walking her to the bus, she starts crying and asking me to go with her. I'm not about to let my baby be alone at this time, so I jumped on the bus with her. We got down there without her father knowing i was coming. The other thing her father didn't know was that he was about to be a grandfather. This was a feat I learned only a couple days before myself. I was going to break up with her, because, to be honest, I had too many women at me, and I wanted to be free to get with them.

Getting in the car, April just started crying, AGAIN. "I'm stuck, because I love April. But I really wanted to be by myself. As I was holding her, and asking her what was wrong, she said to me, I'm pregnant. Now, breaking up was not an option, because I was not going to leave her to raise my child by herself.

Arriving in Kansas, getting picked up by her stepmother, she told us she would handle things with her father. Because, as I remember, as I told you, her father didn't know that I was coming.

April's part Dominican on her father's side. And at the house was a bunch of Dominicans with Uncle Grito pulling up at the last minute, in all black and a ponytail. Pops kicked it with me a little but pushed me straight to the hotel. This episode went smoothly, and we were back on the bus to return.

We had a layover in St. Louis. I was playing the pinball game of Meteor and listening to MC Shan on the Walkman. April was supposed to be listening to the call for our bus loading. She was just as much into the game as I was. I mean, I hadn't played like this in four to five years. Popping credits had the machine humming. By the time I looked up, the whole bus station was empty, and April looking stupid. The next bus wasn't till 11:00 the next morning. So we got a hotel room with our bus ticket stubs.

Getting back after being gone only a couple of days, My connect was in a panic. He was thinking that I had rolled out on him with his lil' money. Life of a hustler! Spend all this time trying to make some money in a life where there is no trust. Oh well, back to getting it.

My Son

With the main spot shut down, and Summer Courts not really doing anything, I had to get out there to sell the dope myself. My decision was to start selling ounces with now having two kilos to work with. Getting spotted one and purchasing one myself, left me without a choice but to trust others to help me sell it. I wanted to give dudes the same chance I got to make some money.

Leslie and I rode around all day, putting things together. I found some dudes to push the dope for me. In my hood was Vincent, Cole, and Rich, my original crew. Down in Summer Courts was Little Man. Now, from there, these expanded to Little Man introducing me to his cousins, who sold dope. And before you know it, if you didn't buy from me, you sold for me, to the sum of $10,000 a day for the Summer Court area.

The shock of my life came when kicking it with Leslie and his girl was over to his house. She started saying things to me like she's seen my son and he looks just like me. First of all, I don't have any kids, to my knowledge yet, so I started getting upset with her, and so did Leslie. That was the way we were. She began to get scared and started explaining that Rachel had a little boy.

I tracked down Rachel's number, and I called the same night, and all she had to say was, "Come see for yourself." The next day, I went and held my boy. He was already six months old. The same day I went, I bought him everything he needed, and then some. This was the happiest time of my life.

Rochelle and April weren't feeling this part of the game. But for me, this meant I had a son. The feeling was having someone to teach to play ball, to live life, and to protect, even at the expense of not knowing how to be a man myself. The pressure of being a dope boy was starting to get to me.

On top of everything, Leslie's lawyer was telling him he was only going to get probation. So on his birthday, he went to court by himself because it was supposed to be an in-and-out thing. The judge gave him four to fifteen years in prison. I got a call from his mom, and immediately, I headed straight down to the jail to see him and find out what was up. Leslie had three women himself to deal with. I brought each one of them individually to the jail just to see him. If they were to get with someone, he instructed, it would have to be me. His main line was off limits. That would just be disrespectful.

Before they sent him off to prison, we had one last visit. We talked about the last time we clowned, which was a few weeks prior. We had gotten two hotel rooms and bet to see who could get the most sex, but not from a main line. He won this one, three to two. I had only one original, and he had two. We switched girls one time, so he had the ups on me.

I also informed him that his lawyer was already paid for and would bring him out on super shock probation. That cost me $3,000.

I spent a lot of time with my son, especially with my partner down for the count. I also started spreading myself more with the ladies, and I was allowing myself to befriend a lot of guys that I usually wouldn't hang with.

I started drinking more, smoking more weed, and smoking more primos. During a visit with my son, late at night, I had been drinking. Rachel and I decided to have sex again. Two sexual encounters, two boys.

Meanwhile, the drug trade was getting even better. I have dope and money at every place I want. My spending habits had risen to at least $1,000 a day on clothes, eating out, buying weed, and treating folks to the luxury of having money. Rochelle's house was still my main spot for housing money and dope. She would stay up late with me counting money. We would cover the kitchen floor with $100 stacks. Before Leslie went to jail, I had bought him a '98, like the one I had. So now, it's sitting out in front of Rochelle's.

I decided to get my Bonnivillle fixed. It had been down for awhile with a blown engine. So I took Rochelle's car without her knowing it and placed her engine in it. With all that was going on, my son was still the joy of my life. I saw him every day, sometimes, two to three times a day. We would go riding, just me and him. How could things get any better?

Allison

Having this load of money had many drawbacks. Now every day, now everybody I ran into, either wanted me to do something for them or with him. With Leslie gone, I needed that one real friend. Lamar, Bryant, Head, every one of my boys, had their own thing going on. So we just hooked up to do things, or to help one another, but I needed that one person, who was just my friend.

Cole and Rich were doing their thing, but we could only do so much hanging out because we had a business to run. Riding through the hood like I did every day, pulling up to the light over on Brooklyn, I see a fine girl coming out of the beauty salon on her way to the phone booth. Pulling up, all I could see was stone wash. The closer I got, the more of her face I could see.

I had the music pounding, so it got her attention. I hadn't seen Allison in a long time. I asked her if she needed a ride somewhere.

"Well," she said, "Yes." Riding to her house, we talked over what's been going on, and what's been happening since we last saw each other. And of course, she has heard about my newfound thing. We exchanged numbers, agreed to see each other later, and then I left.

The strange thing about running into her was it made me think about how we had met. I was fifteen, and she was twelve. Her cousin and I had one of them junior high girlfriend-boyfriend relationships. Also, I used to date one of her buddies.

We had tried to get together for a relationship, but it never manifested. We still had managed to become good friends, to the point where she shared with me the loss of her virginity on the day it happened. I was hoping to get something going with her because she was bad; she was nice. She looked good. So we started kicking it, and before we knew it, we spent a lot of time together. She was quickly becoming that friend I needed. She was the only person at this time who really didn't want anything from me.

Plus, I'm laughing again, not at folks, but with someone. April and I seemed to have a relationship where she was either mad at me or I was mad at her. My control issues has gotten out of hand, and on top of the drinking and drugging every day, I don't get that much rest, because I'm either on the go, selling dope, having sex, or spending money. I couldn't park my car anywhere, because somebody would stop me, either wanting to buy dope or it was some female looking for me.

So many guys were asking for help, I started a half-ounce program, where I would give someone a half ounce. The only thing I had asked them to do was buy from me every time they needed to re-up. Being with Allison was fresh. Nobody knew where she stayed or that we were talking. I could tell her all my worries, stresses, and conquests without her looking at me any differently. Plus, I told her about April, because she was my woman, and I ain't leaving her for nobody.

I've always wanted a Cadillac; that's why I kept renting them. My connect had bought an '87 Cadillac Fleetwood, white on burgundy, with the plain Jane wheels. Soon as I saw it, I had to have it. He finally agreed to sell it to me, for $10,000. I took it straight to Mr. T's, and got some music placed in it. I rode my Caddy like this for a week, and then it was time to throw it in the shop, to get that baby done up.

The money was flowing good, my partner and I would bet $1,000 for the best out of five shots on the foul line. I actually lost a set of Trues and Vogues, plus a grille for my Caddy to him, on the foul line.

There were several things taking place in my life. First, I was so lonely now. Having this money wasn't solving my internal issues. Second, I'd developed a habit. Whenever I didn't spend the night with a female, I would be at a hotel, trying to escape life by smoking primos all night, sometimes not getting any sleep for days.

During the days, there was weed and drinks, with my nights filled with primos and drinks. Allison was the youngest female I was associated with, at sixteen. I could always tell something was special with her, but my life only allowed her to service my needs. After a month of our new relationship, we decided to have sex. Here it is, I have all this money, and I'm sneaking into her father's house after hours. After sex, we only became closer.

Things evolved to the point of my not wanting to give her up, either. To be honest, I wasn't giving Rochelle or April up, because they brought different qualities to the needs of Horace G. While all this was going on, Lyndsey had become an intricate part of my operation because I felt sorry for her. I would see her out at places with the same outfit on, and shoes. She was pregnant, and nobody seemed to want to help her. So I gave her an opportunity to help herself, which really only seemed to serve me.

I hadn't seen my Pops in a while at this point. So when he came looking for me, I was surprised, leaving his number with one of my good friends to call. On a night where I didn't want to be with a woman, or be at a hotel by myself, I called and asked him, Could I spend the night? From this point on, we began to live together and reconnect as father and son, or more or less, Big Horace and Little Horace.

Taking Hits.

Finally, my Cadillac was out of the shop, with $25,000 invested into it; the baby should have been able to dance. Hitting this town with the baddest short-body Cadillac had its perks. This meant a different level of everything: women, riders, and robbers.

So far, I have been coasting, taking minimum losses. Then come losses like $6,000 here, $12,000 there. Everybody's stealing from me, gaming on me. This began to feel like I was hustling, just to pay the money I owe. Cole and Rich both catch dope cases where it costs me $3,000 apiece for lawyer fees, plus the drugs, which were lost in the mix.

A trusted friend beat me for half a key.. Because of my mismanagement of my spending, bills were sky high. I pay everybody's bills and they have jobs. My brother, on his way to jail, decides to steal money from me, making it look like April did it. The only escape I had was a hotel room, with XXX movies and dope.

My father and I became tight, but the resentment of his leaving me was always there. All my friends liked him. He was the type who could brighten anyone's day. This is how I discovered his true feelings for my mom. All these years, there was only one side I had heard, which was hers. He would actually sit there and play "Have You Seen Her?" and cry. And of course, he would be drunk.

Because of my success selling drugs, he quit his job, leaving me to take care of everything. And then there was Tasha, the new girl on the team; we got into a little disagreement, which ended with a car chase. And I wrecked my dad's car. I had to pay for the damage by tricking that baby all the way out. Things were moving so fast I couldn't keep up.

Now, Tasha came on the scene only because of her father's reputation. He was a playa in the streets with a ton of respect. The night my Cadillac got out of the shop, we hooked up. She was impressed. So for the first time, we went out. She asked me on the phone what I was wearing. I told her Iwas wearing a black silk pants outfit with suede shoes. She showed up in a matching silk suede plus jewelry. Now I'm impressed!

So she got close to me, because she had her own stuff, and was bred to be with a hustler. Because everything wasn't the way I wanted it to be on the Cadillac, I only drove it from the shop to the garage until the shop owner was ready to finish it.

Turning in early one Friday night, my partners took the rental Cadillac out for the night. About 10:30, I got a call from my partner telling me to come up to the Pizza Hut on Gettysburg. It's jumping!

Earlier that day, I had Tasha pick up the ninety-eight from the shop, with the instructions to take it to her house, and don't move it.

So I got out of bed to meet up with my crew. Pulling up in the Pizza Hut, with the roof back, windows up, and banging my music on ten, all eyes were on me. Every mouth dropped. People pointed fingers at the man. Bending the corner, looking for my partner, he was parked with the front end ready to roll.

I parked right next to him, Caddy on Caddy. Getting out with the whole parking lot on my tip, we just gave each other dap and a hug, and we just turned, and sucked up all the glory. With a bunch of girls surrounding us, all we hear is a loud system in the parking lot. We both knew the sound of the system. That was my ninety-eight, the loudest and the cleanest system in the city.

Bending the corner was Tasha and a carload of her girls. She backed the '98 in next to the two Caddies, jumped out, and chased the girls off. We posted up for another ten minutes or so. It was time to ride, with me in front, with my partner behind me, and Tasha with her crew bringing up the rear. Boy, that was real living.

Meanwhile, Leslie and I were still in contact. He called everywhere for me. Just like he had put it down to the two of his girls to mess with me? Well, we did that, one more than the other, because I was trying to get paid. Dwight was still around, helping me handle the biggest parts of the drug trade. We would lock ourselves in the apartment, starting at 8:00 p.m. We would break down and rock up, and prepare for distribution, each one of the kilos. This would take us all night, sometimes until six or seven in the morning.

By this time, I'm picking up three kilos at a time. Selling them ounce by ounce moving the total of 15-20 kilos a month. Riding with Rich one night, smoking weed and chilling, we ran out of weed, and couldn't find any. Rich remembered his sister's boyfriend sold weed. So we rolled up there to get some! When we got there, Rich went to the door, and I waited in the car. After being in there for a minute, he motioned for me to come on in. Rich said the boyfriend wasn't home, but his sister offered to take care of us.

Sitting in the kitchen, I didn't know what to expect. I hadn't seen his sister in a long time. She came into the kitchen, and my jaw dropped.

This was a grown woman. Star was at least four to five years older than me. My last memory of her was being chased because I grabbed her butt and ran. We all chopped it up for a minute, then we left. I asked Rich to hook me up with her. He said it was cool.

On Friday nights, my dad bowls in a league. So I go up there to support his team. My partner Dwight bowls on Fridays against my dad, so we would all be up there betting.

Being at the bowling alley was fun and different. My usual crowd wasn't there. For a few hours nobody wanted drugs from me, money from me or women trying to holla. But then, running into a friend of mine's mother one night, we started talking, not thinking too much about it. We talked until the bowling alley closed, being the last two to leave. I could tell she wanted to get with me because while walking to our cars, She then turns to me, and says, "Can I get your number?"

Being in shock, plus trying to honor the game, because I'm like, I've been trying to date her niece for years, selling dope with her sons and nephews. Plus, I still have the relationships with my dude's mother. I respond with, "See you next week." When next week came, I didn't go up there and she managed to get my number from my Dad, and a whole lot more.

This ended up getting back to her kids, and everyone was mad at me. Rich calls, saying Star wanted him to give me her number. I called to set up a movie date. Now, she has a man, and me, several women. So we have "NO"business driving down the main strip in my Cadillac like no one would see us. This was my ego because I know better. Leaving the house to go pick her up, Tasha pulls up. I spun her with a lie and pulled out.

Picking Star up with pride because she was fine, and older, and looked real good in my Caddy. On the way to the movies, Tasha saw us, and started acting a fool. We're in front of the movies, held hostage, because she was trying to run us over. Everyone waiting on the movie was looking at us laughing. Finally, she pulled off, only to go grab some eggs, to egg my car, and get her big brother on me.

Coming out of the movie, I saw her father's truck parked in front of my car. Both doors swung open, and two big dudes got out. They wanted to put their hands on me because I hit Tasha in the eye.

At first, I had know idea what they were talking about. We hadn't fought this evening. But then, I saw the eggs on my car and went straight off. I told them to follow me, while I was pulling my gun out, and I was trying to get them down to the hood, so I can get a good shot at them. They followed me for a while but ended up turning off. Star is trying to calm me down, which I wasn't feeling. I dropped her off, without saying bye, or nothing. This was our first date.

Now I've created a situation for myself I really didn't want, with April, Allison, Rochelle, Tasha, and Star now in a permanent rotation. Then there was my son's mother, Rachel, the bowling alley chick, plus my other activities, being set up by women who are getting sent by dudes after my money. Something was going to have to give, and give it would do.

Coming home to some dudes trying to kick in my door led me to evaluate some things. Come to find out, Tasha had been running her mouth, really being tricked, and another girl gave the rest of the information. After having the locksmith come and fix my door, I was cleaning up, and my phone rang. It was April, asking me if I messed with Tasha. I just said, "Not anymore," while motioning to Tasha to get her stuff.

Having still just my son Damon, December yielded me two more kids. April had our oldest daughter Jalen on the 14th. Then the shock of a lifetime came, Debbie was working at the gas station by my house. I hadn't seen her in awhile. The last time we were at the car wash, she was with her guy and a big belly. I always assumed she was pregnant by him.

Every morning, I usually stop at the gas station to fill up my car before my day gets started. Oftentimes, we spoke. Others, we didn't. This particular morning, she's standing at my car window, asking me to meet her over at her grandmother's house at 3:00 p.m.

I never went, but several days later back at the gas station, she was a little more aggressive with her approach. I agreed to meet again but didn't go. Again, going for gas, she approached talking a little crazy, too. I just asked, flat out, "What do you want?" She said, "I want you to see my son." My first thought was, "Somebody else trying to get some money." I gave her my number and just said, "Call me."

Finally, the year's coming to an end. The birth of my little girl was starting to have an effect on me. Well, that and the fact that all my running around had me up in the hospital with IVs in my arm, from being dehydrated and suffering from malnutrition. With the money and the women, plus friends and all that, the lifestyle I thought would make things better, is turning out to have the opposite effect.

Suddenly, everything is really starting to get on my nerves. I'm tired of hearing story after story of why you don't have my money. Or how you're only buying one ounce because your other money is tied up.

Every week, I'm handing over $72,000 to my connect with the feeling of a stick going deeper and deeper in my butt. And the matter of the five women, who called themselves my woman. I'm having sex with three separate women on a daily basis, just to keep them from whining. Every time I turn around, one of them is crying about nothing. Ain't none of them telling me to get out of the game, or to slow down, they just want to know why was I over here, or over there?

Rochelle and I had fallen out, because she wanted to be with me, and decided to get back at me by messing with some dude. It had to be an issue, because I thought I didn't care about her, not like that, but I did. So I decided to first take her car and hide it. She brought the police to my apartment knowing I got all these drugs in here.

Then I got an idea to jump on her. After beating her up in the car, I took her to the apartment, and we got into even more. Leaving to take her home, her boyfriend, with his friends, were waiting for us. They pull out the biggest gun I have ever seen. The one without the gun was telling the one with the gun to shoot me, because he was tired of me.

While they're figuring out who was going to do what, I jumped in the car, and pulled off. The gun was so powerful that the bullets coming past me are rocking the car each way. Going to change cars and get my guns, Rochelle kept calling me. I wouldn't call back, because my mind was made up. She reaches me from a strange number, with the two dudes with her, everyone saying they are sorry, and, "Please don't get us."

I told them they would meet my grandmother. She was deceased. After this conversation, they called the police, and now I was on the hot sheet for kidnapping and assault. Before being caught, Rochelle and I had made up, and she was back handling my business.

Now, I'm looking at my baby girl and April saying, "I need to get myself together." After the new year came in, I made a decision. To commit to my family, the woman I love, and my baby.

The Bottom Falling Out

Making the adjustment to being a family man without all the extra activities wasn't easy. A lot of the relationships could be cut straight off, but some took time, because they played a part in my business. All the women knew about April and where she stayed, so not hearing from me for a couple of days made them drive by the house, looking for my car. No one ever approached April or her house. They would wait across the street in the UDF parking lot or put notes on my car.

April and I began to talk again, laugh, and have fun. The baby brought us so close together. I decided she needed a new wardrobe with shoes to match, and I went out and got it. A lot of my decisions at this time were guilt decisions, because I knew she loved me with all she had, and I spent the whole nine months she was pregnant acting a fool.

My life had started getting some joy back into it. I had pulled back on getting high and drinking. I wouldn't hang out as much or date other women like I used to. Handling my business took a lot of my time. Me and my Pops hooked up every day, and I spent time with my son, then went back home. April and I would stay up all night talking and laughing, eating junk food. With the birth of Jalen, she had become more demanding in a way that she was stepping up. She would call for me, and I would come. She would tell me to go take care of something and I did.

This was my woman and my family, and it was important. I asked April to marry me. She said yes. We went and put some rings in the layaway. April couldn't drive, but that didn't stop me from going out and buying her a Z28 to teach her how to drive. That was a gift to my lady.

Then it happened. One of April's old friends started coming back around. Before I knew it, April had a list of women and things I had done. We had a big argument, which landed me on the couch of my pop's crib. This really had me shook, because I'm leaving all of that behind. At the time April and I were going through our thing, her mother and stepfather were having problems also. April and her mother both decided to leave us and go back to Kansas.

I walked in the house, everybody looking stupid, saying, "They gone." April had taken our baby girl and left me because of my running around. Instead of continuing to remain strong in my separation from the chaos, I dove straight back into it headfirst. Depression had set on me worse than before. I became careless in a lot of my activities. Tasha was coming around again without the permission of her parents, so she's choosing me over them, which I didn't want.

And finally, after months of giving Debbie my phone number, she calls to arrange a meeting. Debbie is still with the man she was with back when we had sex. They're sharing a house together, raising their kids. She invites me over to her house while her man is out of town, going over there drunk with one thing on my mind. We sat down for a minute, discussing how this had come about. I'm listening but really checking her out, because like I said, I'm only here for one thing. She decides to go get my son to show me, sitting him on my lap. There was only one thing I could say. Either he looked just like me or I'm super drunk.

Turns out little Jamie looked just like me, and there was no denying him. In the meantime, April called me regularly, telling me she was coming home and to send her $500, only to call back a couple of days later to tell me she spent the money so send her another $500. Driving one day talking to her on my cell phone, not paying attention because we were arguing, I tore up the front end of my Cadillac. Even after that, she tells me if I want her to come home, go get another apartment with new everything, because she doesn't want to be lying where another woman has.

So I go get another apartment, buy brand new everything from big screen TV to the floor model in the game room. She still doesn't come back. By this time, I'm over the edge and falling deeper and deeper into the game. I started to try to make some business investments, only to be taken for the money. My crew started to see the weakness in me and had their way with my money. My father started selling drugs himself and was taking liberty at taking dope from me to start his own enterprise. Eventually, he got jammed up by the police, only to give me up. So this costs me a chunk of money to make it all go away for the both of us. Because a lot of the stuff I had was in Horace Gullatte's name without Junior or Senior on them, he was selling my stuff and just acting a fool.

With April being gone, Allison became the one I leaned on. She listened to my problems and acted like she understood how I felt about April leaving me. Spending a lot of time with Allison helped get me through a rough time. There was a small drought at the time, so I wasn't on the go as much. Without a lot of business to handle, I started enjoying just relaxing, going places, and doing things. Lamar and I would take our ladies to the movies, bowling, you know, just hanging out together.

Allison around this time got pregnant. I was happy she was pregnant, because I liked her, and she was replacing April. Somewhere with all she had going on in her life, she chose to have an abortion but told me she had a miscarriage. For a week, she allowed me to console her over the loss of our child. Finding out she lied to me had a major effect on how I looked at her. Then things changed.

Sitting in the house, plotting my next move for the night, a strange number comes across my pager. Calling it back, it was Sasha, Lyndsey's friend. She gives me this rundown about wanting to move out of her mother's house because they weren't getting along, and she knew the apartment next to mine was empty. I wasn't doing anything, so I asked her if she wanted to check mine out to see if she might like the one next door. She said yes and asked if I would come get her. Because she and Lyndsey were so close, I didn't think anything about it. At my apartment, we came in and sat on the couch. It was two-stories, so I only showed her downstairs.

Rolling up a joint from the shoe box that sat on the table at all times, we sat back, smoked, and watched videos on the big screen with the lights out and the blue neon blinging off the phone and the clock. The mood was a relaxed setting. After the weed set in pretty good, she asked me to show her my upstairs. We went upstairs to see my game room, with gym shoes lining all the way around the wall, and my sleeping quarters, which had an impressive bedroom set. We lay down on the floor to play video games. This girl looked like the girl from the Bobby Brown "Every Little Step" video.

The end result was, for a long time she was trying to get at me, and because of my inability to control my sexual urges, we ended up having sex several times, only for Lyndsey to find out. Tasha was on some kind of trip because she won't leave me alone. Maybe it's because I still have sex with her from time to time. She felt obligated to jump on every female she thought liked me. Not only was she driving women away, she threw food at my house and whatever else she could think of.

Without any locks on the windows and living in a bad part of town, dudes had their way, coming in my place. I never kept money or drugs there, but my clothes, shoes, jewelry, guns, whatever they stole. I came home twice to find one dude coming out of my place, and another time, I was coming in the front while they were pulling out the back, trying to fit my fifty-five-inch TV out the back door.

The sad part to all of this is I wasn't happy at all. Constantly in need of some attention was my driving force to continue. My self-esteem had gone out the window a long time ago, with principles that wouldn't stand in any normal circumstances. During these times of everyone accepting my attitude and lifestyle, having some money didn't really cross my mind as to the reason they were doing it. In my odd way of thinking, I thought Horace was the draw and the friends and the girls were here for me.

Obviously, there were those who blatantly tried to play up on things from me, but the reality of this is my main core was the people whom I grew up with, had relations with, and family. Who would ever think these folks would start to resent me because I was taking the risk to make life better for all of us? So secretly I knew or felt things weren't what they seemed. When Mr. 725 came home from jail, it wasn't about him serving me; instead we were on the same team. He could never really accept this, because it cut into his dealings. All I ever wanted was to say I had a kilo, and I had folks secretly trying to take my life, give me up to the police, and find ways to pay me back because I had sex with their woman.

I can fully stand up to admit my sanity had been driven to its limits with the fame, the women, the drug-selling. All that stuff equals nigga rich. My mind was constantly being distorted with someone telling me this or that with motives to get next to me. The pressure of reimbursing my connect's money as quickly as possible and using the drugs, were tearing my body down. In my best thinking, I couldn't come up with the simple solution of placing locks on my windows.

Because it was still a drought and dope was scarce, there was more time to just kick it. My spiral was going so fast that even during the drought, I was losing money. I paid rent at several places, along with cell phone bills and everything else. My monthly get-high bill exceeded the usual amount. My bankroll was taking a serious hit up until it was all gone. Because of my name, I could easily obtain a few thousand dollars when needed. Being in this position didn't seem to bother me, because the money was getting on my nerves, anyway.

What came to the surface was how many people depended on me to eat. I had developed a reputation for helping dudes and not running my mouth about their business. Looking back now, I realize just how I ended up with the attitude that will be displayed in later chapters. One of the dudes from my hood and I started hanging out kind of tight. We both loved to smoke weed and chase women. He was used to messing with a different caliber of women than I, but women are women. My Cadillac was back out of the shop, looking even sharper than before, so on special days we would ride the Caddy and do our thing. A lot of times I did things without thinking, so I was never aware fully of who I was hurting.

Bob and I had met a girl named Mika. She was the type to have a house full of women. We used to pick them up and smoke weed, ride around, just chill. Coming from the skating rink one night, Bob and I decided we were going to put it down on Mika. We had her in the middle, so every time we passed the joint, she hit it twice to our once. Dropping everyone off, first we took Mika to my house. We began to try and get it on with her, only for her to start screaming. I noticed she would only scream when Bob touched her. After several tries, I was like, "Let's take her home."

The next night I went by her house by myself, and she and I had sex. After this, she was looking for more, but never revealed this. The next week at the skating rink, I saw a girl so fine, and she was checking me out. Come to find out, she was a friend of Mika's and wanted to hook up. I asked Mika to do the introduction. Mika didn't believe that Angie and I would hook up. Well, we did. Plus, I ended up liking this girl. The more time we spent together, the more I ignored Mika and everybody else. This is a problem, because Allison was now living with me. April was still in Kansas. Rachel had revealed her feelings to me. Well, her sister told me. Same thing.

My life seemed to be one of running from woman to woman, problem to problem, looking for the answer only I could find. Every woman in my life to this point either left me because of my jealous, abusive ways or just tired of me. My next girl Angie was just another opportunity to mess things up. The best part about messing with Angie, she knew who my woman was, and she had a dude, so we could ride, smoke weed, drink, have sex, and both go home to our partners.

I decided to go down to Kansas to get my woman and baby back. Rich and I took off down there with no driver's license between us. And too, this was another stupid idea. All I knew was what city they were in, We were riding around getting high at the time of this decision. We left Dayton at maybe 6:30 in the evening. After hitting the weed house and drive-through, we hit the highway.

When we started out, we were going the wrong direction. Looking for a divider to turn around, we noticed some kids on the side of the highway. With only three cars in front of us, the kids jet out across the highway playing chicken. Three came out but two went back, leaving one little girl to continue on. Before I knew it, the front car hit the little girl and flipped her high as a building, with her leg slinging out from under her pants. Her leg detached itself from her body. She hit the ground like a rag doll, and our high vanished. We eventually turned around, only to make it as far as Indianapolis. After going to the rest stop to pee, we fell asleep with the car still on. A trucker must have pulled in while we were asleep, because in the morning on his way out, he hit the horn and woke me up.

Arriving in Kansas was uneventful except for the flat tire and that little girl. April met us at a hotel to lead us back to her grandma's. Holding my baby was one of the greatest feelings for me, because she missed me. It seemed like she knew who I was. I only stayed the night, because my tags were expiring in two days. I convinced April to come back. We agreed I would send for them once I got back home. As we started to say goodbye, April, the baby, and I began to cry upon my leaving. Rich offered to drive, since I was in a state.

On the highway, Rich was rolling the Caddy. Obviously he didn't see the state trooper, because he sped past two of them. We got pulled over for speeding, and neither of us had a license. Rich gave the trooper a fake name and Social Security number, but when asked to spell his last name, he couldn't. This landed us both in jail in Kansas City, Kansas. I also gave a false name, so we both down there under aliases. I spent one night in jail for a seat belt violation, and Rich had a $1,500 bond. The sheriff released me without any money in downtown Kansas because I didn't have any ID. My mom wired me $500 at the bus station so I could get home.

Allison found out I was in Kansas because I had to call collect to the house from jail. She then picked me up from the bus station, only to drop me off at the spot we all hung out at. The crew wanted to go to the Holiday Inn and have a pool party. We invited Angie and her crew, plus another set of girls. My partner left and came back with Mika, who thought she would be with me, and I embarrassed her to the point she started crying.

Eventually, April and the baby made it back home, but things were different between us. She wanted me to stop seeing Allison, and I couldn't, because the feelings I had for April had been given to Allison in April's absence. Plus, Allison had become pregnant again. So April and I did nothing but argue, and she wouldn't allow the baby to come with me. Rich was upset with me because I didn't come right back to get him. My mom had to wait a week until she could go down there to pick the car up and get him, so another partner of ours went down there and picked him up.

Meanwhile, life was what it was. Because the drought was still going on, a lot of things had changed. Instead of having everyone spread out, paying all these bills, I had people moving in together and picking up some of the slack. My mom and I move in together around the corner from my son. Come to find out, Debbie's mother and my mother knew each other, so they discussed their grandson all the time. Debbie is bringing my son to see me, but she wants to have sex every time. Rachel had another little boy, and for a year didn't tell me he was mine. I just used to play with him all the time when I was over there.

To me, it was impossible for me to get her pregnant two times after having sex only two times, so I never asked and she never said anything. I just took care of him, because he was my son's brother. Going to get my son so he can take a ride with me, he was asleep, so I asked Rachel if I could take her other son. When I stopped at my mom's job for something, she asked me if this was Jamie I'd brought with me.

I told her, "No, this is Rachel's little boy."

My mom replied back, "No, this is your little boy." After going back and forth, not hearing each other, she picked him up and said, "Junior, this is your son."

I drove straight back to Rachel's house to ask her if this was my son. She wouldn't tell me, but her sister called me stupid and said, "Yeah," so now my total was up to five.

The Decision

By the time my connect got back in the pocket, I was down about $1,500 in bills. Outside of the bills, the time let me think about something. Because I wasn't moving fast, the revelation of how my connect had started acting and some of the things they had done came to light. The discovery of my connects actions hurt me, because I was, for one, loyal to this dude, giving him credit for my success, when in fact I was the one putting in all the work.

There were people, good people whom I could trust, telling me to walk away, but the dude had too many moves. I had become so involved in this situation that I didn't know how to walk away. The end of the line came when he gave me something for $50,000 when it cost $30. Then people close to him were coming to me, because they didn't agree with some of the things he had put down on me. So with all of this combustion and a clear head, because I had slowed my drinking and drugging, I came up with a plan to make both parties happy.

Before setting in on this plan, I needed some time away to really see if this was the right move. A friend, his girl, Allison, and I went to Cedar Point for a couple days. No one had any idea of what I was doing. Coming back from Cedar Point, two things happened. First, my connect was panicking looking for me, which showed a sign of insecurity, trust issues, and guilt. We've dealt in hundreds of thousands of dollars repeatedly, and now it's a panic or so over fifty? This proved to be the deciding factor.

Second, walking into the house, my brother-in-law is sitting on the couch talking about take him home. He lives in Detroit.

My only question was, "Can I get on?"

He said, "Thirty a pop."

So we put the money in the engine and hit the road. By the time I got back in the city, the intensity of my connect had turned up. Without us ever speaking, he had come to the conclusion something was wrong. He and his people were showing up places either before I got there or after I left. Because of my success as a dope man, I had created enemies I didn't know I had. Now my friends didn't want to ride with me.

This beef here was separating me from a lot of people who were in it for the ride. My mission was to flip his money to obtain enough to get my own. Then I would not fall into this type of trap again. But as time elapsed and the more distasteful my thoughts became about these boys, my thoughts went from giving up the money to him not getting nothing. I knew what came with it, I just didn't know so many people would be against me.

I was spending a lot of time on the road, either in Detroit or Cincinnati. My time in the city was spent behind tinted windows and hotels. There wasn't one male friend whom I could trust. Everyone had their own agenda, which I could see a mile off. Allison was my confidant in this matter. Rachel was my rock, and April just flat out was worried about me.

It hit the streets, Horace had gone AWOL from the crew, and they're giving up $500 a pop for any information about my whereabouts. The stress of the situation was building with each passing day. Attempts on my life were increasing daily. Now because of my vulnerability, dudes were taking shots at my mom, not literal gunshots, but trying to break in her house, once pulling up on her and my sister and nephew, trying to force them into the house, but a neighbor saw it going down and stopped them.

Another time, kicking in the door while my mom lay asleep in her bed.

The pressure was really mounting. When arriving at my mom's one night, a truck hits the corner hard. Out jumps my partners and their hired gun. Dwight was with me this time, and he was panicking. A lot of heated words were being exchanged, but my eyes continued to remain on the gunman's eyes. I'm willing to give the money up, but only if my connect comes in to get it by himself. He won't come by himself, so we were at a stalemate. At this point, I was tired of hearing, "Shoot him, shoot him." I put the key in the door to go into the house. This took everyone by surprise. By the time they recovered, I had opened up the door and gone into the house. Dwight was still outside, begging for his life. It's funny. As long as a person can reap benefits without consequences, it's cool, but as soon as it's time to face something, they don't have nothing to do with it.

My addiction had kicked back in big time, which was causing me to slip again. The daytime was the time I would sleep. In the nighttime, I would stay up all night. I was no longer scared of gunshots or even dying. My main mission was not to die and to be smarter than the opposition. Even functioning with limited resources and half the brain capacity, I stayed one step ahead of these boys, for the most part. A lot of money was going into hotels, rental cars, and smoking it up.

Along the way, I still had fatherly duties plus my own shopping. Trading my Cadillac in on a new Astro van was cool, but a bad deal. Even at this point, I could make any move I wanted to make, but my connects mouth just kept getting on my nerves. I began to stalk him but could never get to him. A friend once told me, "It's not about how many people you shoot, but who you shoot, which makes a difference."

Everybody was selling me out for $500 or for free, trying to get in good favor with my connect. Lamar ended up in jail for sixty days or so during this beef. Because of our closeness, he had access to wherever I would be. He called me one night on a three-way from jail. After our discussion, something didn't feel right. I moved into my emergency room next door, just in case. Like clockwork, my connect showed up. I watched him out the window talking mess to an empty hotel room.

On hot and sunny days, I would go to the mall or someplace where a lot of people would be and make a walk-through. Mouths would literally drop seeing me, like I was a walking dead man. My jewelry was still top of the line, and my clothing to match. The same problem I've always had would be my downfall: if I wasn't in Detroit in the strip bars, I was chasing skirt around Dayton and Cincinnati.

The beef between us was getting hotter and hotter, because the longer I stayed alive, the less my connect looked like the killers they professed to be. Those who really cared about me were stressing out every time I walked out the door. Leaving Rachel's early one morning with her two young cousins in the car, I ran into one of my connected partners waiting on me. Because of the kids, I pulled over to let him know we could settle this without the kids in the car. Because he was this skinny dude with a big mouth, holding a .44 Magnum, he just didn't talk right.

I shut the door, and a chase pursued. He ended up in a mess of cars and me still moving. Right there, I decided to get him first. I got caught slipping, and they got me. They got my van and a lot of clothes, jewelry, drugs, and a few more things. My van was burned up on Gettysburg, the main strip in our city, to make a statement. The ashtray of my van was taken to my mother's house and placed in the driveway with some matches.

This beef became an obsession for a lot of people. Basically, the whole time this was going on, my connect and I talked on the phone. Over a period of time, we began to discuss why the other dudes were coming at me so hard. Everyone wanted me out of the way so they could have my spot. Some of them were willing to kill me for it.

April and I hadn't really seen as much of each other, but we spoke a lot. One night on my way to Detroit, I stopped by to see her and the baby. We had sex, and she got pregnant. Finding out she was pregnant was all bad, because Allison had my back through all of this. She stood up to my connect and wouldn't give me up. She wouldn't allow me to ride by myself too much. She was right there and pregnant, so getting this call at our apartment with Allison sitting next to me was hard to take. The next words out of April's stepfather's mouth were, "It's twins."

My world was crumbling fast, and there was nothing I could do about it. Because I didn't trust anyone at this point, I wouldn't sell any dope. I just stopped selling dope but continued spending. The whole scenario was taking a toll on Allison. I could see it on her face. Her family didn't want to talk to her, and I needed her, but her happiness and our child's safety were critical. I decided to call her mother and get them back together. Soon she was back at home with her mother, where she needed to be.

No sooner than Allison went back to her mom's, the beef ended but not before some fireworks. I made the mistake of allowing Lyndsey back into my life. I didn't know she was accepting money from my connect in exchange for my whereabouts. She had given them my number, and soon my address. Lamar and I were riding, smoking weed. We decided to hook up with Lyndsey and her partner. At Lyndsey's house, we agreed that Lamar and I would come back to get her and her friend.

When we pulled back up, I got out of the car and I knew I could see one guy lying in the grass across the street, with one more leaning against a house and another behind a tree. I just missed this because I was high. Before, when we arrived at Lyndsey's, the house was packed. Now it was empty. Just her, no friend, nothing. She told me we would pick her friend up later and to go wait in the car. Leaving out the door, she grabbed me and gave me a kiss. When I turned around, the door slammed, and then the same three figures I thought I saw were standing in front of me with their guns out.

The lead man began to tell me, don't move or he'll shoot me. My gun was in the car with Lamar, and he was in there with the music loud, high, and unaware of what was going on. I just kept saying, "Huh?" until I reached the car, and then hollered out, "Fuck you." I began yelling to Lamar to roll out. We had to back up to them. I anticipated at least the car being shot up. These fellows were more scared of me than I was of them. They ran, then let a couple of shots out as we drove up the street.

After that night, I turned more aggressive in my approach to them. This had to end. Six months has passed, and only God knows why ain't nobody dead. My phone had been ringing for a couple of days, more than usual. My gut feeling led me to believe it was my connect. I picked up the phone, and a familiar voice came over the line. "What's up, man?" We talked for a while and agreed to meet in a neutral place. He was under the impression I had some dudes riding with me on this. He mentioned during the conversation about the meeting for me to leave my boys at home, and he would do the same. Lamar rode with me to the meeting but entered after I did and lurked in the background. The meeting went well, and the beef was finally over. At the end of the six months, my life had drastically changed for the worse. All the people who counted on me to take care of them were no longer able to count on me. My addiction was full-blown, showing no signs of slowing down.

My heart had been hardened, and the fear of dying no longer existed. I felt I had been taken to the brink of my short existence and couldn't no man do anything to hurt me. My thought then set on the fact that if I were destroyed, killed, or hurt, it would be by a woman. My desires to have money, to be a dope man, or to have notoriety were gone. I didn't like myself, love myself, and indirectly just couldn't or wouldn't fight any more for the life that has cost me everything I had.

The most disturbing portion of my feelings came when I thought about my children, my mom, the women who believed I would always protect them. I didn't want to be here. I didn't want to live anymore. But for some reason I couldn't get enough nerve to directly end my life, so I set out on a mission to get something or someone else to do it for me.

The Aftermath

The beef ended just before my twenty-first birthday. This was very monumental to me because I had given up hope on making it this far. Celebrating this day with the guys from my hood only opened up questions about my life and what I had just experienced. My reason for returning to the hood was because I knew nothing else. Soon to follow was the reselling of drugs. Because of my secret addiction, I was unable to really get anything going for myself. I was trying to start over from scratch with too many responsibilities, an addiction, without the actual desire to be doing this. I couldn't pay my bills, so I had to hang out some nights with the fellas until Allison's mom went to work at six in the morning. Then I began hanging back at April's, so between the two of them I would get a bath, some sleep, and something to eat.

Star came back into my life at this time. She was really a godsend because she fully understood what I was going through. She had broken up with her dude and was offering me a place to stay to help me get back on my feet. Moving in with Star was cool, but the problem was I didn't like Star. I needed a place to stay. Star was a good girl who had a big heart, but I'm in love with my children's mothers. I wouldn't even sleep in the bed with her a lot of times. I just slept on the couch like I fell asleep downstairs.

With all these things going on then, here comes Allison's brother, who had a girlfriend who was trying to get me to sleep with her. I wouldn't sleep with her, so she used something she knew about me and April to share with Allison's brother. I kept telling Alex to get her out of my business, but it didn't happen. Riding one night with some fellas, we happened to ride past Alex's girl house with his truck outside. Getting out of the car to confront them, they wouldn't come outside. Frustrated, I began to beat Alex's truck with a two-by-four.

Alex emerged from the house with a shotgun and shot it. He had the gun aimed right at my heart. The gun went off, but it hit one of my dudes behind me. Hearing my dude holler, "I'm hit," shook me out of the trance I was in. We jumped in the car to go to the hospital. On the way, my dude said, "Blaze up the last joint." So we smoked the last joint before pulling into the emergency room.

We had to put him in the door and pull out, immediately going back to the spot to holler at the crew. Cole had just got out of the hospital for shooting himself in the leg. A couple of weeks earlier he got shot in the foot, so he is itching to do something. We loaded up four deep in the car. Driving past the girlfriend's house, as soon as we saw movement, we unloaded, I was sitting on the windowsill with one hand on the steering wheel, someone hanging out the other window squeezing the trigger. We set a blaze to the house and pulled out. The next day everyone was on their way to see my dude at the hospital, but I couldn't go because the police were waiting on me there.

Coming home one night from drinking at the after-hours spot, Star's baby daddy was over, Star and he were arguing. I could hear through the door. I'm not getting involved with that, so I turned around to go back out. When I got in the car, he came out to leave. I turned around to go into the house. He saw me and asked about Rich. I told him I didn't know where he was. He then proceeds to follow me to the house. I used my key to go in with Star still sitting on the couch. I motioned for her to tell him something. He began arguing again, complaining about me. I held out as long as I could, then asked him nicely to leave because it was late and stated he could come back tomorrow. My man decides to come for me only to find the barrel of my gun in his face. This made him start speaking Spanish, walking out backward.

Things are bad. Real bad. Shoot outs, robbing, hanging out on the corner. I'm just out there doing whatever to make it. Star and I are getting closer, but it's still not what it should be. Every chance I got to get violent, I was. Allison had our baby girl, and she wants her independence from me and my violence. She was tired of my mess, I was supposed to be this strong man while in fact, I am this loser who doesn't even have a place to live. She started sneaking around on me with me finding out and putting my hands on her. Which only made things worse.

Life was really starting to be way too much and just having a spiral effect. I was trying to hold on to my life with everything I had. Everything and everyone I encountered just kept going to crap. Star, despite me tearing her car up, I wasn't paying any bills and was sleeping on the couch. This woman was pouring into me when nobody else would. Finally, I came to the conclusion to stop playing games with Star and get my life together.

I started by preparing for her a nice meal to be ready as soon as she got home. I cooked ribs, mac and cheese, green beans and had desert. When she came in, I hugged her and the baby, gave both of them a kiss and told them I missed them. I've never acted like this before.

Star then proceeds to tell me about her day. She explains she went to the doctor, and he told her she had an STD. She continued to say he gave her two prescriptions. One for me and one for her. In the beginning of the story, I thought she was saying I gave her something, but she was saying she had slept with someone else and brought the STD home to me.

That same night I left, leaving behind one of the best women I've ever had the pleasure of being with. Leaving Star's was really the beginning of a couch-to-couch episode that in later times would be a part of my breakdown.

Leslie's mom had been living by herself since Leslie went to jail, so I moved in to help out with the bills and keep her company. Soon after I moved in, his brother moved back home with his woman and three kids. At first things were going OK, but like always, something always goes wrong. It seemed like trouble was awaiting me at every corner. Going to the drive-in landed me in jail. I sat in jail three days with a thousand dollars-worth of dope squeezed between my butt cheeks.

Meanwhile, April had the twins, two baby girls. When I called the hospital to check on them April started crying saying the babies had died. I told her I was on my way to support her. She kept saying, no don't come. I went anyway. Upon my arrival at the hospital, April had informed security not to let me in the room. Security walked me out of the hospital with me believing my babies are dead. At first, I didn't understand the reason for this. I guess, It was already hard for her on her own, and with me in there, it would have been even harder. If my life was already screwed up, now my babies are dead. I would think sometimes that it was for a reason, because I knew we couldn't afford to take care of them, but it still didn't take the pain away of them dying.

At this time I am not running in the streets, I actually live in these streets. Instead of getting money to put a roof over my head or take care of my children. I ended up renting a convertible car running around saying its mines.

On top of this I started taking Valiums with smoking weed, drinking, and primos at night. It's 1991, the year of the NWA Niggas For Life rap tape. Between the drop-top, drugs, and this music, we were acting like complete fools. Rich and I would be together the most, making a full day of hustling, robbing, drinking, etc. We found ourselves in many uncomfortable situations. None more uncomfortable than a shoot-out at a bar. Coming away from that with Rich and I being named as participants, this was only an added problem to everything else we had going on.

About a week later. I went to pick up Lamar so we could go pick up his girl from school downtown. Lamar was driving, and I was in the back seat. I noticed this maroon car following us, but I didn't let it register. We stopped at this clothing store so I could retrieve my watch from a friend. While I was in the store, the police swarmed the parking lot from every angle. What made me turn around was how big the girl's eyes had gotten. When I looked, the police had their guns out on Lamar and his girl. The looks on their faces was of sheer terror. I'm standing in the store trying to figure out my next move. The store manager won't allow me out the back door, so I'm just watching the show go down. After a few minutes with Lamar and his girl in the police car, the police began to look for me.

The security guard from the mini-mall approached, and I saw him pointing to the shop I'm in. This was a woman's store so when the police came in I started looking at clothes like a shopper. The police kept calling my name, but I wouldn't turn around. Before I knew it, they had me on my tiptoes taking me to the police car. They began to question me about a bunch of stuff, even my name. All they had was a description of the car and anyone with the name Horace. I said my name was Bryant Smith. The police were so confused that they began to ask Lamar and his girl who I was. They would say Horace and I would say Bryant. Finally, the police started asking the huge crowd standing around. The people in the crowd even said my name was Horace. The last straw was when the police noticed a bullet hole in the car.

After digging the bullet out of the car, the police were high-fiving and clapping. This is when I stopped being Bryant and became Horace. They took me down to the police station to question me. I asked for my lawyer, but the detectives wouldn't allow me a phone call. Not given a choice, we had an interview. Because we didn't kill anybody, I just told the truth of what happened, which in street terms I still told too much. The police were the ones who did all the shooting that night, and they needed some scapegoats and we were it. Because I wasn't charged at this time, I was released.

The next day I got the car back. Rich was still on the run, and the detectives were in the hood tough. After several harassment run-ins, the police started holding two pictures up in the hood. One of Rich asking, "Have you seen him," and one of me saying I'm a snitch. This began to label me as a snitch in the streets.

All of this trouble caused me to be put out of Leslie's mom's house. My stepmother, who still stayed in the hood, allowed me to use her couch. This was a hard period of life. Also trying to duck the police and deal with now I have a reputation for being a snitch. Ain't this something? I went from being a major player to a snitch without even being charged with a crime yet.

My stepmother was a street person. She began to tell me how to get my life back on track. She told me to get a job and stack my checks, so I went and got a job at Wendy's.

This was my first job at the age of twenty-one. So I would go to work at Wendy's, then go down the street where the fellas were to hustle. Bryant was the only one who would sell me dope because he didn't believe I was a snitch. Everyone else would kick it with me, then talk behind my back. Bryant pulled me aside to tell me don't nobody want me down there because they think I'm a snitch. These are all the dudes that when I had the pack, I helped and made sure they got some money.

When it got dark, all the fellas would hit the clubs, leaving me down there for the customers. This is how I made my money, by waiting until they left, and the customers came to me. I was doing real good, plus starting to feel better about myself. I'm spending time with my kids just doing me.

The job at Wendy's fell through because of my attitude. This left me with more time on my hands, which I filled by moving in down the street into the dope spot, gave me a place to stay and I was making money. Life began to get better for me. But, deep down I knew this was just a band aid. I was still so alone.

In the hood, there's beef between The Shoop boys and the crew on Hoover. At this time I have no allegiance to either side.My dope spot and temporary home is on shoop. One night the Hoover boys decided they were going to rob me. Sending in the decoy first to see if i had some dope. The decoy was nervous as hell and that made me go look out the window. I saw a guy on both sides of the door. While I was headed to the door to lock it. The door busted open knocking me to the floor behind the door. The first guy came in shooting the ceiling. I jumped up, pushed the guy over the table and ran out the door, running straight into one of my homies almost knocking him over with his gun in his hand. I ran across the street through the yards and down to my step mom house. That night Bryant and I rode around for hours looking for them.

The spot got shut down, This began a string of going to jail every month, sometimes twice in one month. Going to jail for domestic violence fighting with Allison or April. Driving without license jumping out the car running from the cops, you name it. Running from the police on one occasion my chest started pounding really hard. The policemen thought I was playing until the ambulance got there and took me off to the emergency. Before I knew it, I'm laid out on a hospital bed with wires all over my body. Come to find out, I had a mild heart attack. The doctor asked me what I was doing to be a twenty-two-year-old man with heart problems. Explaining the type of drugs I was using and the way I used them, the doc asked if I was trying to kill my self?

I continued to take pills, which at this time had escalated to Tylenol Four, a Soma, and a Valium all at the same time. Taking them three times a day with smoking weed all day and smoking crack at night, I was actually out of it. For the most part, not remembering half the things I was doing. I was robbing, selling real dope and fake dope at the same time. It really depended on what pocket I reached into. These were the times I was thankful for a couple weeks in the county to get my head cleared up only to get back out and do it again.

The chaos just kept going. Drunk and high on pills another day, Bryant and I went to the mall, and got thrown out because we were too high. We went across the street at Applebee's. With me getting into a fight. The police came, placed us all in the police car. After hearing our story, they released us, drunk and all. Bryant's so drunk he couldn't even drive. Leaving Applebee's, going somewhere driving fast, the sheriff got behind us and flagged us down. I told Bryant to act like he was sleeping. The story was we were out drinking, and I had dropped him off at home. Soon as I got home, his girl was calling me to come back and get him because they started fighting. That's why I don't have my license on me, and my name is Bryant Smith, and this is my aunt's truck.

The sheriff released us with yet another warning. Two weeks after that night, we were out drunk and high again riding around. Bryant's uncle had a '77 Camaro, like the one I used to have. I had been trying to buy it from him for the longest. We stopped by his house and he told me $500, it's mine. I gave him the money but agreed to come get the car tomorrow, but I wanted to take a test drive. Bryant didn't want to go, but he had to. We ride around the corner and a lady runs the stop sign, and it puts us up on the sidewalk. Since Bryant had licensed, we switched drivers. From this, we both got a couple of thousand out of it.

Now I'm living in hotels paying by the week. Nobody wanted me and my mess around. To escape the chaos of the streets and the crazy dudes, I would go hang out with my good guy friends. These are the guys I grew up with who didn't run the streets. They had convinced me to play on their softball team and eventually got me to leave the hotel and come live with a homeboy of ours. These brothers took the time to show me good qualities and how I can put them to use. I began to study for my GED and look for a job. I stopped running around in the streets and had left all the ways behind.

Going down to the public library to take the pre-GED test and later receiving a pass slip with the opportunity to take the big test one time for free. Also, I had landed a job at a print shop plus working for Cassano's Pizza. I would be at the print shop from eight to four then work from six to close at Cassano's. I had begun to save money again, I felt really good about myself for this. One of my good guy friends Curt was an electrician, and he was going to plug me in with the apprentice position with his company. He instructed me it would be better to get the schooling first, then the field work. This would allow me to make more money. So I went to the JVS, a joint vocational school, to take the test of enrollment. I passed and was scheduled to start school in a few weeks.

While waiting for school to start I get pulled over and off to jail I go for driving with no license. The judge gave me ten days in the workhouse. School was starting in a couple of days, and I could only miss three days of school. In the end, I was in jail again, lost my job at the print shop, and missed all the days I could miss for school.

Addiction

Getting out of the workhouse without a job or school to look forward to did a lot to my confidence. The people in my corner were still trying to support me, encouraging me to stay on the right path. I tried hard by applying at a temp service and went to work at a factory. This just wasn't working out. I flat out gave up and gave in to the temptations and comfort zone of my rigid life. Tired and frustrated, I chose the gun to be my choice of hustle. Because of where my residence was, I could go over to the west side and cause trouble and come back to the east side and relax. My mind started to think about the dudes who used my kindness and friendship for granted, attempting to call in a favor, and all I received was a smack in the face.

This made me go after all the guys who I helped to take the help from them. If I robbed someone who wasn't on the list, then it was just a matter of wrong place, wrong time. A lot of the men I went after were hard for me to get to, so their workers would do. There are many robberies I regret doing. I struggled to forgive people because of what I thought they had done to me. One being in case was my cousin, whom I assumed was working for Mr. 725. I set out to get him, calling him on the phone and setting up a meeting for a couple of ounces to make this thing look legit. I took some newspaper and cut it in the size of dollar bills, making $1,000 stacks with rubber bands around them. Then throwing the fake money in a brown store bag with a Footlocker bag. The meet was at his mom's house, which I didn't like, but that's the nature of the business.

Jumping out the car with this bag swinging, I was greeted with a smile. In the end, I had the dope, and he had the fake money. I never pulled the gun out on him, but I showed it to him. Upon leaving, I told him to tell whose dope it was that I was looking for him also. Along the way, I had seen another guy who worked for a guy I'd been looking for. Pulling around to Bryant's, there was a group of guys chilling in front. I stayed in the car for a minute, drinking and popping pills, overhearing the worker explaining that he had got the stuff on him. That made my attention go up. Like usual these days when I pull up somewhere, everybody seems to have something to do, leaving with the one guy who trusted me the most, Bryant.

I sat there for a second contemplating whether to take this lick off. Finally decided to do it. I just got in the car with Bryant knowing just what I was about to do. Rolling up on the worker, instantly coming up with the pistol out in broad daylight. I had him naked on the street. Everyone was watching me like I was crazy. And, I had to be out of my mind to believe I was robbing guys now for pay back or for money.

During these days, my addiction was only getting worse. Depression was my partner. Low self-esteem was my best friend, with lack of confidence running a close second. Crack cocaine became my everything. The uses of the other drugs were the mirage for those I would be around. I spent days in the house smoking dope by myself. Eating very little, getting little rest. When I would come out of the house, it would be to get something to eat, to make another lick or to sell some dope. My lifestyle wouldn't allow me to go around certain people because I was ashamed of what I had become.

Sitting in front of Smoke's aunt's house talking to some of my homeboys, a car pulled up asking me could they holler at me? It was two major dope boys in the car questioning me about the words I spoke to my cousin. It turns out the dope wasn't Mr. 725; the dope belonged to these two guys. One of them I had helped out when things were good on my end and bad on his. All they wanted to do was talk, but I ain't trying to talk. My attitude flared and my pistols came up. These boys pulled out hard with my homeboys running on me.

I was really finding ways to distance myself from people. Folks were trying to reach out to me, but every time, I would let them down. Just like I wanted it to be, I was all by myself. Everyone was getting on with their lives, and I was stuck in the past feeling sorry for myself. Having nowhere to go with no money and now without a pistol because I got pulled over right in front of the halfway house trying to go see Leslie. So now I have a CCW. While in the county jail for the gun, April tells me Leslie tried to make a play for her. By him being my boy, it was cool with me. I would rather it be him instead of another dude.

After getting out, I conveyed this to him, which in turn he shot back at her. Come to find out he was salty at me for having sex with his girls and not sending him money continually. I'm beyond caring about everybody else's feelings because I'm homeless, broke, and trying to survive an addiction, which has taken its toll on me. I don't go around my children because I couldn't buy them things I used to. So now I'm hanging back in the hood on the block. It's wintertime. I don't have the clothes to properly dress for the occasion. One thing I had on my mind was coming out of this rut.

I didn't like being in this situation. Because the block was slow, and it was cold, it would be hard to flip a $50 double up in a day. My goal here was to hold on until something broke good for me.

Every morning, buying a double up, just to buy food, plus getting cheap hotels for the night and do it all again the next day. Sometimes things would be so slow there wouldn't be enough to get a hotel room. That's when I used one of the emergency places I had to stay the night. Even with all that Bryant and I had been through, he was right there for me. His house was one of my emergencies. Because I had some pride, I refused to just lean on anyone. This was a very hard time for me, but this is where I had to dig in.

My reality was starting to unveil itself with every day I would spend out there on them streets. No matter how much I wanted things to be different, they simply were only a result of my actions. It hurt me a lot to see all those around me who struggled because of my inability to sustain things. I didn't have the desire to be a dope man, but I didn't have the faith in any of my other abilities to change my situation. My children's mothers are constantly reminding me of my lack of being a provider and how I made my bed, now I need to lie in it. All of them are involved in other relationships, but I still remained an important part of their lives. During the times where I couldn't buy a hotel room and nearly had smoked all my product up, I could call Lamar anytime and he would either give me some dope to get back on my feet or just get me a hotel room, get me something to eat and stay hanging out in the room with me for a while before leaving and picking me up in the morning.

Bryant would do the same, whether it would be to keep me at his house or take me to get a room. Both of them knew I was going through a rough period and never came down on me about my actions, but always tried to encourage me by letting me know no matter what, they had my back. The nights I would walk the streets with nowhere to go and my pride not allowing me to reach out to anyone. Those were the loneliest nites. The fight for survival brought me to total irrational thinking.

A Couple of brothers robbed Lamar with the first person he called afterwards was me. All of us are from the same hood and grew up together. We even share common interests in girlfriends and baby momma's. Lamar is my guy, so I Had to ride with him. For all the respect I thought I had, My best friend is asking me to kill another friend for him. What made matters worse, Lamar decides to not keep this to himself. Walking the hood late one night cold, hungry and looking for a place to go. My homeboy pulled up and asked me to ride with him to make a sale. Riding to meet the guys, my homeboy told me the plan was to rob them for their money. When he told me who it was, I didn't want to do it because the dudes were cool with me, but I never asked to get out of the car. Sitting in the backseat thinking about my life and how I got here. And, then I remembered why I was in the car. To handle something Lamar won't do himself. On top of this my friend is offering me $500 to do this. My life was worth $500, ain't that something. After the group met up to do the exchange, come to find out the other guys were setting my homeboy up for the robbery also. A few shots got exchanged leaving one shot and one robbed. After leaving the scene my homeboy pulled over in the alley and put his gun straight in my face. We wrestled for a moment with me getting out the car standing there looking at my homie. He stated he couldn't believe I was riding with Lamar.

When things got too hectic, I would go down to Cincinnati with my mother. This was one of those times I stayed down there for a couple of days and then came back down to do battle. Things were kind of heavy because the guy I was supposed to see knew about it and the dudes from the other night were looking for me. Just another day in my chaotic life.

Moving on from this mess, I was starting to see my boys by Rachel. Rachel was and is the coolest one of my children's mothers. She would be mad at me for not spending time with the kids instead of what I could buy them. Rachel and her boyfriend were having problems and to make him mad, she would use me. I came over to see the kids with Rach asking if she could go to the store. She instead goes around to her boyfriend's house and ends up in a car chase with my car being the one that got torn up. The car wasn't totaled, but it wasn't the same. I had also started sleeping over Bryant's mom's house on the couch. This was cool because we were like family, anyway. I never planned to be living there, but circumstances forced this. After tearing my car all the way up, leaving another person looking for me, I continued to stay at Bryant mom's, but went to the hood to sell my drugs every day.

Slowly, however, I stopped going to the hood and worked off my beeper. My addiction was full-blown. Pride held me together enough to let me keep a decent appearance so many people couldn't tell how serious my problems were. Still, no matter what, trouble couldn't elude me. A friend of mine introduced me to a friend of theirs who liked to get high. I would extend credit to these people, only to the strength of who they knew. Running out of money one night, I was offered a $250 money order for the front of a $50 rock. If my money was not there in twenty-four hours, the money order was mine. These people didn't show up for three days. When they did show up, dude had another money order for $250. This time we worked out a good deal for the money order, and then he told me what was going on. His brother was like a district manager for a chain of convenience stores and somehow had gotten control of a money machine. He wanted my help in cashing the money orders the next day. I called my partner Reggie, who was down on his luck, and we all went out to get that money.

Something that guy said to me made me mad, so I took all the money and money orders from him, putting him out, leaving him with just bus fare only. I gave Reggie the money orders, and the rest was mine. That's how that went. Bryant's mom and his sisters had this cookout party where they were selling dinners. Everybody showed up. There was gambling, drug selling, drinking weed, smoking, you know, same shit. My homeboy Jack Shaw was over there gambling with the old school hustler who worked for Mr. 725. J Shaw ends up losing a bunch of money to this dude, but it was on an IOU. That same night, Bryant and the other Bryant both had their cars stolen. The next morning I was awoken by Bryant and Bryant talking about they knew who stole their cars.

Come to find out a very close friend to all of us decided to make it happen. I get up to assist my dudes. Getting in the car, it's four guys and one gun. They give it to me. We got most of the stuff back and grabbed a close friend. Things happened, but we didn't really hurt him too bad. The same day J Shaw came to get me because Mr. 725 was talking slick to him. We went to meet him, and his dude was shocked, both of them, to see me with J Shaw. This changed the conversation a lot because Mr. 725 was a dude I had already had problems with and by this time I'd had good run-ins with Mr. 725. My reputation for causing trouble had grown strong. The agreement was for both of them to bring $50,000 a piece, winner take all. J Shaw wanted me to rob the whole place and split the money with him. I was robbing the place and not giving nobody nothing.

Rachel was dropping the boys off and not coming back to get them for days and weeks at a time. This gave the boys and me time to really bond. This is how my youngest boy and I became real close. He never wanted to go home. When Man-Man would go home, Dre' would stay with me. Bryant's little sister had a cookout for her birthday party. For the cookout, I would grill all the food out back by myself, drinking a beer and turning meat. This female came back there and just started talking to me. We talked for a minute before she asked me do I remember her? I didn't know this female from Adam, but I remembered the situation. Continuing to talk, she tells me she has a man but will call me if I wanted her to.

We talked on the phone for maybe a week. Then she called my beeper one day. She told me her dude was in jail and wouldn't be getting out for a couple of days. She invited me over, and we had sex. We talked but didn't see each other anymore. Allison and I had been arguing real tough. It had gotten to the point of me wanting to seriously do something to her. She had begun messing with a dude I didn't like, and she knew it. Like usual, she was lying to him and me about everything. My partner, Chris, called me one night. Dude over at Allison's right now. I'm stone cold drunk and ready to act a fool. By the time Chris got there, I'd fallen asleep. I got up and went anyway.

Pulling into the parking lot, I observed these people sitting in the car. Not thinking, I ran up the steps with my heart pounding. The door was unlocked, so I walked right in. The living room was empty. This made my heart pound even more. The thought of seeing a woman I love in the process of having sex would have been too much. When I got to Allison's room, she was in there with the baby putting her to sleep. Instantly, I felt wrong for how things have been playing themselves out. Just seeing my daughter made me realize this had to stop. Allison was terrified, but all I wanted to do was talk and come to an understanding about where things stood. See, I knew it was over and that we were hanging on to something which was obviously causing both of us so much pain. When she isn't in my life, I do good. When she is in my life, everything is bad.

I asked for her to come out in the living room with me just to talk. At this time, her cousin and friend came bursting in the house. The cousin started screaming something about me not doing this while her son is in the house. All I wanted to do is talk, no trouble this time. There was really a reality check seeing my child. The cousin proceeds to the phone saying she is calling the police. This made me pull my gun out on her and made her put the phone down. Trying to control my anger, I said it again, "All I want to do is talk." I then gave the cousin my gun to prove I didn't want any trouble. Before I knew it, they tried to creep out the house on me, and I lost it. I started jumping on Allison and even hit my daughter in the process. Snapping back to reality, hearing my daughter yelling, I just took off back to the car.

When I got down to the parking lot, Chris was parked next to the car with the three heads in it. I was coming toward the car, the three-headed car started pulling off. This made me suspicious. So I kept walking toward the car. The car kept pulling away from me. Come to find out this was the dude I was looking for, and Chris had set me up for this.

The same night the police picked me up because the cousin turned me in. I sat in the county jail on $100 bond, which I couldn't pay. Wouldn't nobody come and get me. Lamar, Bryant, everybody was tired of me acting a fool and not getting my life together. I tried to call Allison and she wouldn't even accept my calls. April won't talk to me, better yet, she has moved again without telling me where she is. And Rachel ain't got time for me and my mess. So I'm stuck in the County thinking of someone to call and remember the female from the cookouts phone number. We started talking and sharing personal information, but she would make calls from me to other women.

The cell I was in was restricted for felonies only. I'm the only one in the cell not going to prison. The sheriff's nickname for this particular cell was Baby Saigon; it was wild dudes in the cell, and I fit right in. I was down for not allowing the police to come in the cell for nothing, and all who went against the rules got jumped on or sent out of there. During the day, I would work out and play cards plus watch *The Young And The Restless*. At night, I would talk to my girl from the cookout. Since the phones rolled all night, one call was all I would need to talk for hours. Also on my calling list was Allison's cousin.

Calling Ms. Cookout, one day her dude answered the phone. She wasn't home, so he and I started talking. She had told the dude we were cousins, that's why I was calling there. When the dude asked me about this, I laughed and told him the truth. I admitted to sleeping with her the day he went to jail. My man started crying to me, all I could say was, it was his woman and if he loved her, forgive her. Getting off the phone, he promised me he wouldn't do anything. I couldn't reach her until two in the morning, she told me the dude jumped on her real bad and she called the police plus had to go to the hospital. Her baby daddy was in the cell next to me and was trying to put a plot together to get him when he got to the county jail.

I had been in the county jail for thirty days before having to go to court. The night before court, I called Allison's cousin, and, in turn, called Allison. I pleaded my case to no avail. The next day, Allison and her father were there to lock me down for as long as they possibly could. I walked out of the courtroom with six months in the workhouse. Returning to the holding cell with the rest of the dudes waiting to go in front of the judge, this guy slides up next to me asking if I was Horace Gullatte. I said yes. His response was he was the one who was with Ms. Cookout. This only made me more upset than I was. I cussed him out bad. It made him get away from me.

The same night I was driven to the workhouse to serve my six months. In my mind, this was the last straw for Allison and me. My mission was to come into this ready to clean my act up. Again, the problem was How do I do this? Not knowing what to do, I did what I always did. Straight into the dorm, lifting weights, talking junk, and letting it be known I'm Horace Gullatte. I hooked up with a guy named Frank who was in there doing six months for the same thing. Also in there was a guy who shared a pretty nice reputation himself in the streets, and he had gotten six months for the same.

After leaving the intake, I was placed in the bullpen, dorm C, which was the farm workers' dorm. Cigarettes went for $10 a pack, $50 a carton, three goodies for a roll up, five goodies for a single. Weed and crack were also floating around for money. The white boys had the action on lock in C dorm. These boys ran who worked on the farm, and all the smokes and the drugs went through them. The main guy became my dude because he either cut me in or we tripping.

Ms. Cookout was right there for me, dropping off my cigarettes and weed, plus we had become real tight. She was investing more feelings into the relationship than I was. My mindset was the same as it was when we first met. Plus, I was still trying to deal with my feelings for Allison. In the meantime, Allison's cousins had been telling me all she could on Allison because they fell out. It was really nothing to me. I was just talking to the cousin because I was locked up.

After being there two months, Allison had gotten in touch with me and we were talking again and she was coming to see me. Ms. Cookout really wasn't coming to see me anymore. With one visit a week, Allison was getting that. I also was handling my business as far as getting weed, cigarettes, and my goodies stash tight. The staff was loving me, and the rest of the inmates were respecting it—well, except one. The dude with the nice reputation was having a problem because he thought I was stepping on his toes, so he started forming a Horace G. hater club.

Working in the social service office, I got hooked up with the St. Clair Community College man who comes out to the workhouse to help folks get their lives on track. Because the workhouse is an opportunity place, you can get work release, school release, or furloughs to handle some important business.

My social worker hooked it up for me to receive three eight-hour furloughs to go down to the college to take a test and register for school. A CO and I had become real cool; as long as he was on, I could do anything I wanted to do. It was evident because I walked the halls like I owned them. Frank and I were busy in the weight room getting swole. At this time, I only weighed 154 pounds. This was the biggest I had ever been in my life. The female COs were super cool and some, I would get on their nerves, their whole shift. Mr. Reputation was getting very frustrated with everyone screaming *my* name and not his. He and his boys were for one, starving, and for two, sick of me. Finally, without words, it went down.

Me and Mr. Rep got to fighting, but the police came before we could really go all the way down. The next morning I pull into the med bay to receive my vitamins. Mr. Rep pulled in with one of his boys and swung on me. I got to hitting this boy so hard, he couldn't do nothing but hold on. Because I was in flip-flops and he was in gym shoes, he had more leverage. The lookout called five-o, and we broke up with me heading to my locker to retrieve my gym shoes. I headed back out to get it on. Mr. Rep jumped behind the

CO, and the CO started talking to me about my furlough coming up the next day.

Ms. Cookout picked me up from the workhouse and took me down to the college. I was down there within three hours, leaving time to spare. Going to the house to call Lamar so I can get to Allison, Ms. Cookout got an attitude and left. I spent some time with Allison and stopping by another friend's house before returning to the workhouse drunk with weed stuffed between my butt cheeks.

The next furlough was two days later, and it took less time to take care of business at St. Claire than the first time. Lamar picked me up and of course we went by Allison's and also by Ms. Cookout's to spend some time with both of them. I returned to the workhouse like before, drunk and weed between the cheeks. My social worker informed me that I would be receiving another furlough in the weeks to come for school business. Meanwhile, I'm running around the workhouse just doing whatever I wanted to do, getting on people's nerves.

The first shift bullpen CO's made the job coordinator place me on the outside gang to work. This kept me away from them except on the weekends. I tried the farm first but wasn't down for pig and cow's mess. So I went to the city beautification, which was cool, but where you want to be is on the paint crew. This was a select crew because the supervisor will allow you to have your way. My first day out on the paint crew, I took $120 out with me to buy everybody lunch. From there, the supervisor and I got real cool.

Mr. Reputation had come off the dumb stuff, so to speak, but that's as far as it went. My homeboy, Larry, was in there with me riding all the way. This time turned out to be more harmful than anything. On my next furlough, all I had to do was sign some papers. Ms. Cookout picked me up and gave me her car to handle my business. She cooked a big meal for me of steak and mac and cheese with a salad. I was supposed to come right back, but I ran around trying to get all I could get, having to be back at 5:00. I got to her house at exactly that. She again had an attitude because I wouldn't allow her to come see me, and I wouldn't write her back, so she just went and got her boyfriend. She still stayed in my corner, but she knew I wasn't for the right thing.

After finishing my time on the paint crew, having sex, smoking weed, drinking and eating out every day, finally it was time for me to get out. I got out about a month earlier because Allison went to see the judge to get me out. My mind was made, I still wasn't messing with her.

The Day

Wednesday afternoon, coming in from work, the Sergeant told me to pack it up. Frank got out early the same day, so we both agreed to hook up the same weekend. Going to the house nothing had changed. Folks lying around, nobody doing nothing. Lamar came and got me, and we rolled around smoking weed, the usual. Because earlier the same day I got released, Ms. Cookout came to the paint site to have sex with me. So, In that department, I was cool. Bryant came by the next day to tell me he was moving to Atlanta with his girl. We went to pick up her engagement ring. This being my best friend, we had to have a talk to see if he was sure she was the one.

He was giving up everything for her and turning straight. This took a lot of courage for him to do this. Being honest, I didn't have the same courage to do the same. He sold his last package of dope, leaving me the little which was left over. Believe it or not, this was a blow to me because this man had been in my corner and vice versa our whole lives. Now he was not only leaving the game, moving to a new city, but he was leaving me behind also.

At the house, I wouldn't answer the phone and had everyone saying I wasn't home. I was trying to straighten my life and stick to my guns about Allison. Because she hadn't heard from me in a couple of days, she did some checking and ended up in front of my house.

Bryant's little brother was out front and told on me, so I had to come out. She was looking so good and acted very frisky. She was demanding to see me that night. And when she wanted something from me, she knew how to get it. My problem was I couldn't just have sex with Allison because of my feelings for her. She, on the other hand, could. So that night, we got together to have sex, and we got drunk, which was something we would do together. After getting dropped back off to the house, my other girl heard I was out and came by to give me some. Just like that, things were back the same way. I had come to the conclusion I couldn't sell dope because of my addiction. Because of me being incarcerated for a few months, the deception was in. With only three days back out on the streets, though, I was back smoking cocaine.

This led to the same cycle as before, going to hotels to smoke in peace. Most times by myself to masturbate to the X-rated films shown at the sleazy motels. Also, the relationship with my dude's mother continued. The only difference was the way I viewed my life. April was working at a grocery store, so I went to see her. She gave me her new address and phone number. This is how I realized for real what we had was over. She had respect for me as her child's father, but respect for me as a man and even less as her man, was out the door. Rachel was leaning on me a little more to be there for her. Not as her man, but as a friend.

This is when I realized she was the woman I should have been with this whole time. It was too late and obvious by her actions. My feelings for Allison were still strong, but in order to have a relationship, it would have to be friends only. I had to accept she was having fun doing things she hadn't done because she was tied down with me from sixteen to nineteen, and now she had a baby to carry with her.

My struggle with my addiction continued. To escape the drug scene, I would contact the temporary services and get work. Like clockwork, things would be OK, but then I was back to smoking primos behind the house. Self-pity, low self-esteem, lack of confidence, all my troubles back invading my life. Things got worse when Jalen asked me for a Starter coat for her birthday. I had the money to buy it when she asked but went on a smoking spree just before her birthday party. Instead of showing up like a man, I didn't call her or go to the party. This was December 14th, and by Christmas my situation was even worse, so I didn't buy the kids anything for Christmas. Rachel was a true friend because she knew I was struggling with a lot and never complained. For Christmas, she just asked that I come and spend time with the boys.

By now, all my energy was gone. Lamar came by and wanted me to go out and celebrate New Year's with him. We went out to club Spunky's and had a good time. Drunk, Lamar lashed out on me with tears. He said he was tired of me living like I was living. He was tired of defending me to people. He spoke on how he used to look up to me and how I made the way for a lot of the homies to get on. This in turn made me start crying. That night I couldn't sleep, just thinking about what Lamar said and how my life had turned around.

Every major accomplishment in my life, Lamar and Bryant was there. When my family stopped accepting me, they never stopped. When I finally graduated at the top of my GED class, they were right there to watch me walk up and shake the mayor's hand and get my diploma. My first shootout, my first thousand dollars, whatever. So this demonstration by my best friend was taken to heart.

My birthday rolled around on January 19th. So far in the new year, I hadn't really attempted anything. I had made a promise to myself while being in the workhouse, no more guns. This is the only promise I hadn't broken at this point. On my birthday, I drank a forty ounce to celebrate turning twenty-four. To me, really, each year I survived was a blessing because the streets had me dead every summer. Lamar came by like always to take me out to smoke weed and to eat. The whole time I was upset that I couldn't even buy myself a nice time.

That night, I laid on the couch shedding tears because I had finally gotten tired of living like this. I began to call out to God to take me away from this life I was living. The answer I got immediately was to get off my butt and start doing the only thing you know how to do. The next morning, I went back to the block without a dime in my pocket. The first day, nothing happened for me, but shortly things began to turn around. It was a slow, hard grind. I was standing on the block all day and selling by my beeper all night. The problem became my addiction, which ate up the profits, so I came up with a plan to stop buying drugs at a certain time so I wouldn't have nothing to carry home at night. This meant only selling on the block. If I had something left, I left it on one of my good guy friends' porch until the next day.

I was finally fighting back, and it felt good to be strong. My will for living and my confidence was starting to come back. I had no desire for a woman, and I wouldn't accept help from anyone. As time went by, dude's saw my dedication to getting my life together and started stopping on a block to holler at me. They would ask me to get in and ride around to smoke a joint and give me the big baller spiel. I started using all this to my favor.

They would be like, "I can do this for you and do that for you."

I would reply, "Just fade me for my money."

Whether it was $35 to $200 because they wanted to appear big, they would throw me swell just to tell someone what they did for me. I had three dudes who I rotated buying from, so I would keep the love coming.

My confidence was soaring because I had a plan to change the way I was living. I was tired of smoking, tired of somebody's couch, tired of not having a place for my kids to spend the night. My life as a whole was a mess. More nights the tears would come down because this wasn't easy to do. I had never felt as alone as I did at this point in my life. By March, my routine was to grab $55 every morning on my way out the door, five went on my two-piece snack from Famous Recipe and to buy a Snapple's fruit drink. The $50 is what I started with each day buying dope. The reasoning for this was as long as dudes thought I was down, they would continue to flaunt their superiority over me. By the end of the day, I would have $200 to $300, depending on how good it was going. The next day I'd start it all over again.

Allison would call me to hook up and have sex or she would stop by on the block to see me. I really wasn't feeling her. I loved her but had found something else that was more important to me, which was getting my life together. Plus, another situation was brewing. Allison's cousin and I had been calling each other since I got out of the workhouse. She was telling me everything she knew about Allison, their conversation. She always liked me. Allison had told her about how the sex was, and she wanted to do it. Eventually, we hooked up and did it. Right after we got finished, I realized one thing about Allison; she was only doing what the rest of the females were doing. Her cousin called her a hoe and whatever else in the book to me just to get me in the bed.

April and my daughter had forgiven me for the birthday incident and started allowing me to come to spend the time with Jalen. April had started dating some guy, which really didn't matter to me. I went to see Jalen one night with him there. April spent more time in the room with us then with her boyfriend.

A friend of mine had introduced me to a Puerto Rican girl named Janet. He was dating her roommate, so after leaving the block, I would go over and hang out with them. Janet and I were cool, but things couldn't get anywhere because of my mindset. Being with Janet was relaxing. We'd play cards and smoke weed. This was a different setting than what I was used to. Everything around me was so intense, so to be in an environment like this was helping me escape the pressure I was under.

The weather had started getting better. It went from being warm one day to cold the next. The drug selling was cool to get me a jumpstart toward a better life, but I wanted more. I was constantly praying to God to come and intervene into the mess I created. My only reason for selling drugs now was because I didn't have anything, not a place to stay, not food to eat, nor clothes to put on my back. My priorities were so mixed up that I only had several pairs of underwear, so selling drugs was all I had.

Coming into the house from just copping some dope, I ran to the room to cut it up, preparing to sell it. Something took over me because right in the middle of cutting up the dope, I swept the dope into the baggy, slammed it into the drawer, and dropped straight down to my knees and started crying and praying for God to come and get me out of this life. Back on the block, things were going well. I had customers. The fellas were back out. Even the girls were coming by. All this wasn't phasing me because of my mission. I got so serious that when dudes would come to kick it with me, I would ride with them for about twenty minutes tops, and then tell them to drop me back off. I wanted out of this mess but had to bear with it until something broke for me.

Riding with a friend to check out a job prospect, we both got hired to be security guards. I received my assignment and got a uniform, ready to report to work on Wednesday. Well, Monday afternoon, Lamont, the barber, stopped on the block to holler at me. He was trying to smoke a joint and let me know the new weed he had. One of my homeboys pulled up and he and Lamont got into it. They began to call each other names. Then Lamont reached for a gun. This made my homeboy dart across the street to retrieve his pistol. When he brought his out, this made Lamont jump in his car and pull out. We all laughed about it and went on with our day. Later that day, Lamont drove back past, stopped at the light, and we all laughed again and gave a pound.

A week went by without hearing anything about the incident. I awoke one morning to sunny skies and a sense that today will be a good day. I left the house at my usual 11:00 to 11:30 in the morning, stopped at Famous Recipe, then moved over to the store to buy a Snapple. While eating my chicken outside of the store, I noticed this female looking at me. When her friend came out of the Sub Hut, she began to tell her something and then they both were looking. I felt it. Maybe it was time for a shape up because I hadn't been thinking about a haircut; I had been just throwing on a ball cap and rolling. There was a barbershop between the Sub Hut and the store. I asked the barber if the chair was open.

The man butchered my head. This made me mad, so I had to fix this. Going to the hood, I passed by all the screaming customers as I tried to get down to the barbershop to have Lamont fix my hair. When I stopped in, Lamont wasn't there. The rest of the shop started talking about the incident because two of the barbers were in a car with him. While we were talking, laughing at the situation, Lamont pulled up. By this time I had started letting Leroy cut my hair. Leroy and I used to be best friends back in the day. Lamont came in, saw me, and instantly blamed me for what happened the other day. He stated that if it wasn't for him stopping to see me, things wouldn't have happened.

He started voicing how upset he was at me and my homeboy for pulling the gun on him. My reply was, "You pulled the gun out first." Which he had done. Now he wanted to fight me. I told him we could fight after I finish getting my hair cut. I also told him he knew I was a warrior. In return, he decided we needed to fight right now, so he sucker-punched me while I wasn't looking and hit me with a combination.

As I spun out of the chair to face him, he caught me with another shot. This made me rush him to try to slam him to the ground. That allowed him to grab me around the neck and choke me. He was trying to throw me to the ground, but that was the last place I knew I could go. The size difference here was unbalanced, with me being five-feet-six and back down to my original 140 pounds and him at least six feet and 190 pounds or so. He began to get tired because he was just holding on to me. The talking trash began. Soon as I felt a little looseness on my neck, I snatched his legs from under him and slammed him on the ground. Now I'm on top of him while he's kicking like a little girl. Because of the choke hold, my blows aren't so effective.

A kick snuck in and knocked me back. While I was running back up on him and pounding his head, he still was able to get up. I proceeded to place him in the same headlock he had me in. He asked me to let him go, and I did. My reasons for not going to the extreme was because Lamont and I were supposed to be cool. My two boys have been his customers since their first haircut, so I thought we were just fighting like dudes do and shake hands afterward.

When I reached out to shake his hand, Lamont knocked my hand away. For me it wasn't any need to be mad, so I got back into the chair to finish my haircut. Lamont then grabbed my pager and slammed it on the ground. I laugh at him and pick it up. He's now running around the shop talking about he going to do this or do that to me. In the meantime, Leroy was in my ear with, "I see you still got your scraps and I know you coming back."

Lamont then stepped in front of me for some more. I just told him I don't want no trouble. He then tried to slap me. I caught it like something out of the movie and said, smiling, "I don't want no trouble."

After more minutes of him throwing threats, he then slid by me again to hit me with another combination. Honestly, I didn't leave because I knew he couldn't beat me. I took his best shot straight up, and he still ended up on his back. My cockiness cost me, and I regret not leaving after the initial fight. So when he slipped past me again, it didn't bother me, but the shots were harder than the first ones. All I did was throw him off me and look at him. This was the moment he had to be looking for with me because it was the beginning of this whole fiasco. He made the statement about making a reputation off me. I fought hard not to get mad. I fought hard not to fall away from my mission. I fought hard to keep the promise I made to myself. After the last shots, he was locked in, and nothing or nobody could stop what I felt he had coming.

Right after the last punches, the police came into the barbershop. The first thing they said was, "Horace, what are you doing down here?" These were the regular police who patrol our neighborhood. My hangout was down farther on Hoover, not up this far. The owner pointed out I was the one fighting, which they could tell by the knots on my head. The officers asked me who was I fighting, and I said he was gone.

The owner of the shop spoke out, saying it was Lamont. Lamont began to tell the police, "Fuck this dude; I am going to serve him every time I see him."

The police left and waited in the patrol car until I got finished with my cut. I jumped on my bike, and the police rode up on me asking if it was over. I went down to the store on the block to get a Snapple and the gun kept on the block. While sending my young homie to get the gun, more homies started coming around. They wanted to go back to the shop and smash Lamont, but I wasn't there. The young homie came back saying he couldn't find the gun. So I went around to see my cousin, and he wouldn't give me a gun. He and his boys started joking with me, and I left.

I went to see another homie; a couple homies were chilling on their porch and spoke to me. I asked them if they had a gun. They gave me a .25 automatic. My bike paddle was stripped and came off as I started paddling away. After slamming the bike on the ground. I headed toward the barbershop on foot. Coming through the chicken joint parking lot, my homie who all this was behind tried to stop me but quickly got out the way.

All I could see in my head was them fools laughing at me while Lamont pranced around the shop talking mess. These images only fueled my anger. Back at the shop, I pulled open the door with the gun down to my leg. Coming inside the shop, I couldn't hear nothing or see anyone but Lamont. My rage was silent and controlled. Walking up on Lamont with the gun pointed at him, he kept ducking behind a customer in the chair. I can't even remember what the guy looked like, and I didn't know his name. Because I couldn't get a clean shot at Lamont, I pointed the gun at the person sitting in the chair. This made the customer duck, and I pulled the first shot. The first shot caught Lamont in the shoulder and made him run from behind the chair. I followed Lamont in the sights of the gun. I squeezed the trigger one more time, and I heard a holler which snapped me out of my trance with me still squeezing the trigger that had jammed.

PART II:

Becoming a Man

County

I bolted from the barbershop with the vision in my head of Lamont on the ground hollering and blood coming from his head. I ran down and through Westwood Park into a backyard where I stashed the gun. Jumping the fence to run across through the alley, I could already hear sirens. Because I had on two shirts, the top one ended up in the trash can, leaving me wearing white and blue instead of all blue. Coming to the top of the alley, I noticed a friend's car in front of her house. I pounded on the door, and Michelle opened the door just in time. As soon as I got in the house and looked out the window, the police were at the corner looking at the house. Sirens were everywhere, helicopters flying above, and I was sitting in Michelle's house with her looking at me like what have you done now? My adrenaline was flowing so hard, I couldn't regain control of my emotions. Real soon sanity prevailed, and I soon knew this time was different than all the other times. Replaying the events in my head of what took place, I couldn't come up with any way out of this. My justification for doing this ungodly act was that Lamont had put his hands on me. I was never scared of anything he said or could have done. I did believe deep in my heart he would try something when drunk and with the odds in his favor. This was Lamont's MO.

Feeling the need to get out of the hood fast, I called Lamar on his beeper. His house was right around the corner from the shop. On his way to answer the emergency code, he rode past the shop and saw the frenzy.

Calling back, his first words were "Did you do that?"

I responded with, "Fuck Lamont; he put his hands on me."

There are a lot of things folks don't understand about me during these times. Nobody knew I was a push away from turning my life around for the good or the bad. I had nothing or nobody. All I could do was protect me and my dream of turning my life around.

Lamar picked me up with the intention to take me to Cincinnati with my mom. I knew I was on my own with this one. So, I told Lamar that I couldn't go down there, and I had nowhere to go. We went to the drive-thru to grab some beer. Intoxicating myself was the only answer I could come up with. That and getting my clothes out of the cleaners. We rode around a while, talking and trying to make sense of what happened to me. Lamar was hurting for his friend but understood the way things go. He knew Lamont and what he was capable of doing when he was with his boys. So we both agreed on my choice and the outcome I was headed for.

I was really in shock. At 11:00 a.m. I was a happy man on a mission. By 12:30 p.m. I was a wanted man on the run. Lamar dropped me off over to Rachel's house to try and get my head together. While sitting there, a news flash came on about a man who had been shot at the barbershop. I was sitting on the floor playing with Damon and Dre', my sons. Rachel's sister London was sitting behind me. The phone rang once, and someone told London that Lamont had been shot. She got off the phone telling me what was said. The phone rang again, and now the bomb dropped. London fell silent, I could feel her looking at me. I turned around to see tears forming in her eyes. We went out back to talk about the phone call. While out back talking, a car pulls up. Doors slammed. It's Rachel rushing home after hearing a story that it was me that got shot. She was relieved it wasn't me shot but sad that it was me about to go to jail.

Later that evening, I ended up over to Janet's, her roommate the only one home at the time. We sat down and rolled a joint and talked about silly stuff until Janet got home. About an hour or so later Janet comes in screaming, "Girl, guess what? Lamont got shot; that's what he get for doing the things he be doing." I just sat back and allowed them to continue with their conversation. We hung out for a while, then went to sleep.

I woke up the next morning with Janet already gone to work. Her roommate cooked us breakfast, then I set out on a mission to do who knows what. In my mind, a shoot-out with the police was the only way I was going down. Accepting this meant no holds barred toward nothing and nobody. For real I was confused and left with nowhere to go but jail. Nobody wanted to be bothered with me or allow me over to their house. The two days I spent on the run were probably the loneliest forty-eight hours of my life.

By later that evening, I got in the car and started riding around. I went back to Janet's to see what they were doing. This time I was met at the door with attitude. Janet and her roommate both felt I was wrong for not telling them it was me and for shooting Lamont. How quickly things change.

Finally, I turned into a friend of mine's house, so only one person knew where I was at. About 3:00 in the morning, I got a call to come to the house. I got to the house thinking it was important only to discover it was a setup. I fell asleep on the couch and woke up to a flashlight and a gun in my face. In the police car, I asked how they knew I was there.

The officer responded with, "Someone called in a tip." The officer also said they were not really sure the tip was real, so they only brought two cars. This occurred around 5:30 a.m., and by 9:00 a.m., I was arraigned on Felonious Assault, and I was on every news channel locally.

To me it was a relief to get a bunk and lay down to assess my current state. Immediately, I had come to terms with going to prison. I figured on doing at least five years. Accepting five years in my mind allowed me to handle what I was facing just a little better.

Allison and I were on OK terms only as parents. She initially told me she wasn't going to be around to do this time with me. I sent a letter to her speaking about how I felt about us and some of the things I regretted, and I wanted to say bye. I knew I wasn't getting out. Instead of moving on, she took account of her actions.

In the cell, things had already started to unravel. This older guy had the cell on lock. All the extras, he ran the TV; he had the power. This got under my skin after a couple of days. I began to do what it is I do: getting frustrated with myself and needing someone or something to take it out on. The older gentleman had to find him another cell to run.

A group of us guys formed a clique and started our time, which had prison written all over it. All of us in the cell were trying to find a way out of the lives we were living. You can know things are not going so well for you, but when you get to jail you quickly find out how bad things really are. The fighting, trash-talking, taking commissary, and the constant bullshit made the staff break the cell up. They sent me to a six-man range. At one time, all six of the men on this range were going to prison with me receiving the least amount of time, five to twenty-five years.

I was in jail with no possibility of getting out anytime soon. The things that were said quietly have started to become public, like my crack addiction. How about the fact that Janet's roommate's baby daddy was dating April? The roommate was always extra nice to me. I never tried to get with her but always knew it was there if I wanted to. After finding out about the baby daddy issues, it explained why she was half-naked that morning cooking breakfast.

All the guys I didn't like or who didn't like me came out the closet and now I am better off in jail than on the streets; I guess I was about to get handled from what the rumor is. My children's mothers were getting on my nerves talking about each other to me. A weekend didn't go by without them being at the club together. I would know who they were with, what they wore, and who they were talking to.

Nique was one of my cellmates in the beginning. His woman was friends with a girl I used to know. With Nique on the phone one night, he said my name and girly wanted to talk to me. This girl and I were real tight for a minute at a time when I needed someone. We began to talk on the phone, but she was trying to get too serious. She would call my other friends in the beginning, and she was starting to catch an attitude. I wouldn't allow her to come see me because of Allison.

The saying "what is done in the dark will reach the light" is all the way true. Allison's cousin somehow thought it would be better that Allison knew about us. When asked about it, I lied. But then there wasn't no sense in it, so I told the truth. This caused a deep separation between Allison and me. She was no longer taking my calls or coming to see me. This went on for a month. I had a newfound respect for Allison. She came to me to put the bad behind, but this was not the time. The mistake was trying to be together instead of friends. Because of our already bruised hearts, every argument and disagreement or bad thought always went back to unresolved issues.

During this time in the county jail, I learned more about Allison than in five years of our prior relationship. My lawyer had wanted me to take a deal, which was hard because the offer was more than I felt it should have been. Plus, when you're still in the county, you still believe you have a chance of getting out. The county jail is also where I discovered who cared about me and who didn't.

I began to pray more in the county, not for a release but just to guide me through this. My mind kept going back to the times of my begging in tears for God to take me away from the life I was living. My understanding wasn't really sure prison was the way he was going to straighten things out for me, but I did believe with all my heart God could make it right.

The female I met through Nique was getting on my nerves, so I hooked her up with a young guy in the cell. Things went really well with them, so they got married. April had gotten pregnant and wouldn't tell me. My daughter slipped up and told me. The funny part is the same amount of months I was in the county were the same amount of months she was pregnant. This affected me a lot. I never thought she would do something like that. Maybe I thought she would never move on.

With my court date lingering in the near future and all my continuances used up, prison wasn't too far away. I had no idea what prison would be like outside of the stories I had heard. The idea of being away from Allison and Toby for five years didn't seem that appealing. Allison was standing in there so strong for us. Her goal now was to keep our family tight despite the past. On her end, it wasn't easy because everywhere she went, someone was telling her to go on with her life. Dudes were all in her face promising to make her life easier, women were in her face swearing they were telling the truth about me. Her family didn't agree with her being with me or that they didn't want me in our daughter's life. She had to sneak to just be in my corner. So the pressure on her was coming from everywhere and would have broken a lesser woman.

Finally, my court date came. I was going to trial trying to win a lesser charge. Allison had to be at work the first morning, so we agreed for her to come the second day. While waiting to choose a jury, my lawyer approached me with a good news bad news situation. The bad news was the judge agreed it was aggravated assault, but since I had to win this in trial, my sentence would be the max with a gun spec. The good news was that the deal of five to twenty-five years for attempted murder would bring me home in three and a half years. Needless to say, I jumped on the five to twenty-five attempted murder.

Soon as the hammer dropped on the five to twenty-five, I heard keys drop. Turning around, I saw Allison had snuck in and was stunned. Knowing she was about to lose her friend, her child's father, and her lover was a terrible shock. She came to visit me as soon as I got back to the cell. The tears on her face said it all. I had to be strong for the both of us, but I wanted to cry also. That evening, I called my mother and father on the three-way. They both began to take claim as to whose fault it was I was in this predicament. As much as I want to blame someone for why I have had such a rocky road in life, I can't. The truth be told, there are things that just happen that we can't control, and then there is the fallout from some decisions we have made. We all have a choice!

Prison

Prison is the only place you will find victim after victim. In the beginning, my thoughts would stray to blaming my victim, parole board, white folks, parents, whoever. Somehow being cut off from society, living day in and day out in a tin can with other men with similar attitudes will have a person believing they are the ones being victimized. For every one man who actually wakes up to the truth about himself and his actions, there are thirty still resigned to a mode of self-pity. I served ten years for my crime because the law says that I am supposed to. Truth of the matter is how can I complain about the ten years when my victims wear permanent scars? So in reality, I got the better end of the deal. I served ten, and Lamont is doing life. If there has to be one knock on the prison system, it would be the lack of understanding the officials have for our being cut off from society. The system doesn't make men better, but it makes them unaware of what real contact as a man in society is like.

Granted, prison is punishment for wrongdoings- and should be in place. If you were to check how many men serving time actually get out, then check how many return, the system will have you thinking those men are just bad apples. To prepare a man to go back into society after ten years, they ran a pre-release class that lasted two weeks. I wasn't taught how to function in society nor shown potential stumbling blocks outside of the normal mishaps I've already encountered. How am I going to care when the folks assigned to look after me don't? I happen to be one of those who was able to get in touch with himself and understand both inside the cage and out. Because I made it doesn't make me any better, and it doesn't make me lucky. No one chooses to reoffend; things happen and there is no other way out and no other way to handle rejection, being shut out, shut down, and lonely. Because those who feel just because they haven't gone to jail, they're better off. Plus, throw in the fact of forgetting that they also were once in need of a chance. The ex-convict running up against those odds will lose. We need not just one chance but chances continually to prove ourselves. A lot is expected of a person leaving prison. One of them being a man! If a person has grown up in prison where he is really dependent, how is he going to really function being independent? No matter how hard he may want to be this strong man, the truth is he will have to learn. The only way you will learn anything is by trial and error.

For me, prison life was like living in an abnormal situation trying to make it normal. Upon entering the gates of the reception center, prison was just a word. The first gate opened, and the van went through like it had done so many times before. When the first gate shut behind us, all I can remember myself saying is How am I going to get myself out of this? Between the gates, the guards handed over their guns and the reception guards shook the van down, looking under the van, under the hood, etc. Going through the second gate meant this is real. Once inside the reception center, we were placed in a single-file line and stripped naked one behind the other. At this point, I knew it was time to suck it up and get ready for whatever. We got processed into the system, ran through a series of tests, got classified, got haircuts, and then sent to a unit. After being in the county jail for six months, I could tell that most of the guys who were down there are at the reception center. The only difference is it was a mix of guys from all over Ohio. This is only the reception center, so everyone here was waiting to get shipped to their apparent institution. After being at the reception center for thirty days, I was shipped to (OCI) Orient Correctional Institution. The move started at 7:00 a.m., and we didn't get to

Orient until 5:00 p.m. that evening. Orient was just across the street from the reception center.

Getting to Orient was a trip. Once we got there, the guard gave us his speech. He said it's gangs and drugs. And you need to buy a heavy-duty lock because they steal. Going over with me were four other men, all white guys. Three of them ended up getting turned out. Orient looks like the park side project in my hometown. When the man said gangs, drugs etc., I was like, I am going to like this place.

After sitting for a while, we were sent to the chow hall to eat. Everyone knew we were new because of the jumpsuits. From the chow hall, we were sent to the intake dorm. Carrying our locker boxes to the dorm, bodies were all over the place. Dudes looking to see if it's anyone they know or checking for other reasons. Being my first time in prison, I didn't know how big everything was. The dorm was big, with long hallways and dark inside with dudes sitting everywhere. When I found my bunk, it was a trip because on the bottom bunk was a bunch of pink stuff, towels, blanket, shower bag. I walked past the bunk several times. I knew what the pink stuff meant, and I was hoping this wouldn't be my cellmate.

Soon after putting my stuff away, in came my homie Nique. He had been there three days or so but looked like he had been there forever. Nique took me around, introducing me to the rest of the homies. In prison, your homies are your allies, especially in a place far from your city. There was Half Dead, Mark, Laudie-Doddy and Hank. Being that this was an old prison and in Columbus, the average age was maybe thirty. There were only six homies in my age group over the whole prison of 2,400.

My first night was crazy. It was a Friday, which meant late night, when we could stay up to 2:30 in the morning. When the gates reopened, it's a mad dash to the phones, TVs, and to grab whatever you may need to watch the weekly movie. I decided to take a walk through the dorm. Going into the basement, the first thing I noticed was the smell of wine, then the smell of weed hit me. Walking down to one of the rooms, I noticed men in makeup and tight clothes, dudes were running in and out the bathroom with these men. Continuing on down the hallway to the rec room, there were pool tables, ping pong, cards and a big dice game. The next room was the movie TV room full to the max with guys watching the movie. In the sports TV room, there were guys watching the movie and some guys cooking hamburgers on a homemade grill. Taking all this in, I felt somewhat at home. The only thing that would make this time hard to do was being away from Allison and my kids.

By my first six months in prison, I had managed to get blessed in properly as a Gangsta Disciple, broke into the top Puerto Rican's locker box and learned how to gamble with cards. Allison was around, but she was having trouble handling the five to twenty-five years. I didn't make things any better because I called all day every day questioning her, trying to basically control her from prison. Also a big load of homies my age came in with one being my cousin Tweet. The old school dudes were taking every dime I had on the card table. Then there were the guys who were locked up with my brother, and because of him, they looked out for me.

My first shank was a piece of iron sharpened at the end to a point with tape around it for a handle. This came about after I broke into the Puerto Rican's locker box. He was talking about killing me. At the end of the six months, I was kicked out of 7 house and sent to 6 house.

I was busy trying to earn my stripes in prison, plus deal with the stress of having my family out there without me. I had really decided to stop messing around on Allison. The problem was I just didn't trust her, so it made me pull away from the other women I was in contact with when things were good, but as soon as things got hard, I didn't have enough faith in us to see it through.

Adjusting to this lifestyle was not easy to do. Soon I started medicating myself as much as possible just to make it through. By now, I had started getting tattoos all over my body and trying to learn games old convicts laid down. I began to press Allison to bring me drugs inside the institution and began to rob dudes for weed. I was trying my hand at pretty much everything to stay busy. Prison life turned out to be no different from the life I had just left. The only thing my life now had that the one on the streets didn't is a consistent place to sleep. Orient was nothing but a big playground for everyone. I was lifting weights, getting some size, and turned to a straight ball head. I got into fights, arguments, and disagreements all the time. I have to say, there were many times I found out I wasn't as tough as I thought I was. I just couldn't beat everyone I faced, and these dudes didn't care, just like me. I learned this quickly and adjusted my game to thinking my way through situations.

Being involved with the drugs, wine, and gangs introduced me to those who were similar, and it was many of them. Everyone trying to come up off each other trying to escape reality. My associates became dudes who did it all. I was an impressionable young man who was seeking approval. So a lot of the things I would do would be to get approval from my peers. Crack cocaine and heroin were also a part of the drug trade. Everything comes in stages, but when you're trying to constantly make things happen, bad things will happen.

My main man "Q" taught me how to play poker. This may have been the single dumbest thing I have ever done. The poker crowd was a bunch of thirsty men who were trying to survive in prison by the turn of the card. One day you could hit for three boxes of cigarettes and lose it right back the next day. Very seldom does a person ever have all that he loses because there is a paper which creates an owe sheet. This presented the biggest problems: everyone always owed everyone.

After a year into my prison term, I filed for probation to get out early. When I was denied the chance, my hope went down the drain. Allison had started to seek comfort in other relationships. I believe this was the moment we both started giving up.

My addiction was still in place, and it was weed and wine whenever they were available. To supply my weed habit, I would run a game on the weed boys. To get cash for your product, you would use what is called a send out. This could either be sent to your affirmed address or western union. At this time there were so many dudes trying to slang weed that you would receive the weed and an address with them expecting you to send the money. Because I would roll by myself to make these deals, dudes always thought I was on the up. All I would say is it was sent. Then if it got too hectic, violence would be the alternative. There were times when I found a guy with some good green and fat fifties and plugged all my fellow scam boys on to him. Every day inside our block five of us would agree to meet up in the spot after 9:00 count to smoke. Some would have the same weed or there would be different. This is where we also exchanged information about who got what. Stone-cold, strong-arm robberies took place also. In a lot of these cases when a white guy is involved, a brother will try to come to you to get the stuff back. I ran this game until I ran into one dude who just wasn't going for it. He put me in my place a little and charged me double; it took me six months to pay him.

My quest became to get my own package; this is how you make the money.

Allison was still coming to see me all the time. The visiting room was sweet. Each month, she would come down and stay all day. My first time getting my own package, my bunky told on me the next day, and I went to the hole for seventy-five days. Before going to the hole, I had become cool with this white guy named Porter. He was very smart and taught me a lot about doing time. He had been locked up for twelve years at the time. The part of prison he understood the most was that, inside, whites were the minority, and if you wanted to have stuff, you needed the right friends to keep it. Even though we both knew we were being used, a bond was formed.

I had never been down in the hole before. It was just like being in the compound except no phone or TV. The porters in the hole come straight to your cell to drop off your package of cigarettes, coffee, candy bars, Jolly Ranchers, whatever your boys on the compound would send you. Plus, you could pay for extras on the food. I began to cell with a dude who had been locked up twenty-three years already. He was seventeen when he got locked up, been on death row, and probably facing the reality that he was never getting out. He began to school me on a lot of things I was trying to do. He had good and loyal friends on the compound, so celling with him meant my time would be comfortable with weed, food, radio to listen to the NBA finals. Even in his forties with all the time he had in, he still had an ear to life. He taught me how to get smart, educated, ready to handle life after prison. In return, he just asked for my youthful energy, my life experiences, and for me to remain thorough. In prison, nobody does anything for nothing. Dudes who do a lot of time live their life through guys who just came off the streets.

After my hole time was up, I was sent back to 6 house. Immediately, Allison sent me a food box and some money. I had just received a clothes box before going to the hole. Within two weeks of getting out of the hole, I went back for disrespect. After serving ten days for this one, I was moved to 2 house where the nickname for this dorm was "Freakin' is Good." This dorm was full of drugs, wine, gambling, and homosexuals. The majority of the dorm woke up at 11:00 a.m. We would stay up all night getting high and gambling, then sleep all day. Things got so bad or were going so good, I wouldn't call home or write letters for months on end. I had obtained a gambling football ticket and a wine business. I was still working out daily and running with the gang. Time was flying by so fast that I hadn't noticed what was really happening.

April had started writing to me talking about God. She had made so many changes in her life since my incarceration. At this point, I was a mess and knew it. She still had feelings for me and was willing to be in my life. Because of the way I was living and the way she was living, I couldn't play with her emotions anymore. I know longer wanted to hurt April. So I stopped writing her and let her go. Inside, I felt worse than I did before coming to jail. I was torn between giving up what I thought made me who I was and doing the right thing. `

Before long, the administration came and broke two houses up, dividing us over the compound. I was sent back to 7 house, which meant more people to deal with, bigger dorm. I lasted several months before getting placed in 8 house. Eight house, at the time, was the hardest block on the compound. The nickname was The Dawg Pound. This unit was filled with gangs, drugs, wine, and every prison con known. While 2 house had a lot of older inmates, 8 house was all young inmates. If you weren't claiming folks, Crips, Bloods, you were claiming your city. Either way, everybody was up under some clique. When the wine would come off, some violence would soon follow. I found myself in the middle of gang disputes involving knives instead of guns. Having two family members, Tweet and Freddo, in the dorm with me made for easier times and harder times mixed together. Both of them happen to be GD also. We also held it down on the homie side. In the sleeping area, it would be based on what clique you were with. Each bay had a letter for identification A through E.

In 1997, I had eight months to go before seeing the parole board. I hadn't slowed down on the things I was doing. I was still receiving visits from Allison and Toby,By now, things had changed for me. I realized I never really knew Allison and the person she was becoming I didn't like. Because of the baby and the fact if she wasn't around my time would be harder, I kept telling her I wanted to be with her. There became times I would tell her I wanted to be friends, and she would go off and make me feel bad. In many ways I treated the relationship like a friendship, anyway. By June 1997, things in the block were hectic. The staff was struggling to maintain control.

On top of this A-Bay was cleared out and replaced with all gangbangers, drug dealers, and wine makers. We lived this way for a couple weeks. Then the officers came and started moving guys out to replace them with guys for a program. This was some kind of drug program where you wore a jumpsuit for an allotted amount of time without your regular living stuff. Day two of this transition, things really got turned up. Inmates who were in the hole were being beaten and forced to come to this program. There were eleven of us who hadn't been moved to a proper location yet. Day three of this transition, we all were being walked to and from chow in a single line with guards. Inside the bay, we were locked down the rest of the day. The eleven of us who were just there because we'd been forgotten about just had to deal with it.

Day four came with dudes getting very hostile because the majority of the guys in this program didn't have a dirty urine or had already served time for a drug offense. The guys started threatening to burn the place down if the officials don't get this straight. They gave them until 3:00. When that time came, nobody came to talk to these guys. They climbed up in the ceiling and started a fire. While up in the ceiling, a bottle of wine was found. So while these boys were tearing up the bay and setting it on fire, a few of us were drinking the wine and smoking weed. As the flames started getting stronger, the sprinkler system was only squirting out rusty water. The guys inside the bay had pushed all the beds against the gate so the guards couldn't get in, but when the smoke started getting strong, the beds were slung from in front of the gate. The guards began to handcuff guys before letting us out. A call came over the radio to let us stay in there: "They started the fire, so let them burn in it." The guards stopped handcuffing us and backed away from the gate. We began to ask to be let out, and the female guard looked at us with tears in her eyes and said she couldn't. Guys began to kick on the emergency door, which wasn't moving at all. There was a window being fixed that had plastic over it. The gates that were supposed to keep us in became the only way out. Kicking on the security gate, we flung it open, and it dangled by one screw in the concrete wall. Inmates began to jump out the window into the grass. The remainder of the dorm had been brought out the other emergency doors and was sitting in the grass already. Every time someone made the jump to the grass, cheers would go up. Since I had my clothes, blankets, radio, etc., I threw all my stuff out the window first, then I jumped. From this point, only one guy couldn't jump out the window. The emergency door was opened for him. We were taken to medical to make sure we didn't have injuries. After several hours of rowdiness, the tactical team came in, and things got serious. The game changed, and the guards took back control of the situation. We were marched over to entry, stripped, and placed in jumpsuits, and put straight on a bus.

All the way down the highway, it was noisy on the bus. When we hit the turn coming down the stretch to Lucasville Prison, every mouth was shut and every eye wide open. Lucasville was one of the most notorious prisons in Ohio and in the United States. Gun towers, walls, barbed wire. We were in shock. As we pulled into the prison garage, we saw a group of guards awaiting our arrival with a white shirt leading the charge. Just by the look of them told us this was not Orient. The white shirt stepped on the bus and quoted the same statement. After saying, "Don't talk, and if you do, we will show you where you are at," they led us off the bus. Placed in a single file facing the wall with our noses on the wall, we were ordered not to turn around. The process of running us past a medic, getting us dressed, and taken to our cells began. I was the last man to reach a cell on cell block k4. Walking past every cell before my own, everyone was asleep. We stayed in Lucasville for a couple of weeks before being sent back to Orient. Our group was under investigation until they found the guys who started the fire. As soon as the officials found out who started the fire, we were released from investigation.

I got back to Orient as things tried to return back to normal. Tweet and I began to do what it is we do. We had an agreement to split everything we got fifty-fifty, which worked better for him because I got stuff from home and he didn't. My parole date was in a couple weeks, and I got picked up for investigation by the institution. Another guy was picked up as well. We both had to see the parole board, so we went in shackles. We both received a sixty-day continuous. After leaving the parole board, I learned the plan of the institution. Going straight to the Rules Infraction Board to be found not guilty and let go back to the compound.

1997 was my first year playing sports since being locked up. I was locked down, unable to really be a responsible man and reap the rewards of being one. Sports became like an alter ego for many of us. Reputation means everything in jail, so being known as one of the best in any sport gets you extra privileges. My main sport was softball, but I was equally as good at football. I became the number one first baseman in the camp as well as the top flag football rusher.

While on the sixty-day investigation from the parole board, Tweet and I began to work our game strong. Things began to bubble, and our names got hotter than usual. We had a homie who worked as a guard. He paid me to beat up another inmate who he didn't like. I'm a convict and would never flip on another convict for the police, so we ran the scam on my homie together. We pretended like we had the fight, and both of us split the pay, which was five boxes of black and milds.

For me, the scam turned into the press game, and my homie had to keep paying me every week. Lying on my bunk next to Tweet, I had just gotten back from getting another payment. Tweet and I were just talking about things. We only had three bags of weed left, and cuz had them. The guards rode down on Tweet, asking him to step out. Cuz started trying to hold the guards off and handed me something. One of the guards blocked me off. Tweet took the bag back from me. Now it's a tussle with Cuz slinging the bag across the bay. The weed went one way and the big bag went another.

I moved quickly to step on the weed, and another inmate grabbed the other bag. The guards cuffed Tweet up, taking him to the hole. I went straight to retrieve the knife he kept in his area. Before I could grab the battery charger for the cell phone, the guards came back to secure the area. Needless to say, Cuz went to the hole for a while.

After my first sixty-day invest from the parole board, I went back and received another one. I'm a little apprehensive about my

146

outcome because rumorville has it after one invest your out, after two who knows? Football season started, and I broke my hand on the field. While the cast is on, I get into a fight. One of the inmates named Big House tried to sneak freak me (grab my Butt). I was trying to fight him with one hand and got busted in the nose. The homies got involved after that and beat him down so bad he couldn't leave his area. If anyone had seen him, we all would have gone down. The parole board was only a few weeks off. I had to feed this big guy for a few days in order to keep everyone out of trouble. From the nose shot I took, I received two black eyes.

Going back after the second sixty-day investment, I received another one. This had me and Allison tripping because we were making plans to start our life over. By the time my next hearing came, I had to be threatened to get there because I was asleep. This time the biggest blow I had ever received came my way. The parole board gave me five more years. All I had in at this time was four. So receiving five more broke me down. I walked around the whole day in shock, not talking to anyone, just in total shock. I called home and told my mom and Allison what happened. They were just as shocked as I was. Allison gave me the best words anyone could have told me: "The world will not end in five years, and I am riding with you." Later the same evening, I went into the case manager's office and broke down and cried my heart out without never telling her what was wrong. As soon as I got myself together, I told her thank you and walked out, still without saying a word.

Sixty Months

February 1998 is a time I will never forget, for this was the greatest test of adversity in my young life. At twenty-eight years old, I was forced to get a grip on my wild ways and figure out why I received five years from the parole board. Up to this point, I believed that I was right for shooting a man who put his hands on me, threatened my life, and had a gun of his own in his barber desk. I had to come up with some answers as to why this happened. For thirty days, I wouldn't smoke any weed or drink any wine. This was a time for me to figure some things out with a clear head. Coming to the conclusion that no matter how I tried to make my hurting someone right, it just wasn't. I stopped believing that I was scared of him because I wasn't. The truth was, I was trying to check out and didn't have the courage to place the gun to my own head. Things between Allison and me were OK, but she began to stress she wanted me out. Lawyer-talk began between the two of us. Myself, I didn't believe a lawyer could help me, but for her sake, I went along with it. In May of '98, we began to search for a lawyer who could get me out. We found a good one who was promising to bring me home if he could get my previous filing of super shock probation thrown out.

The cost was $3,000 for super shock and $500 to file the motion to overturn the first ruling. Allison had half the money, so I called Lamar for the rest. I initially had them put $250 a piece together because I still didn't have faith that I would get out. About a month and a half later, it came through in our favor. It was time to drop off the $3,000.

From the time of the filing to the time of the ruling, Allison had spent her half of the money. Before she had told me this, we had called Lamar, and he dropped his $1,000 of his $1500. Allison wasn't working at the time, and with the baby, I couldn't be mad about her spending her half. With her in my corner, I could make more happen than by myself. With Lamar's money, I went to another inmate who handles his business. Because of our relationship, I received a really good deal to work on making the remaining $1,500 to give to the lawyer. For a street $100 block of crack cocaine and an ounce of weed, he charged me $400. The crack I got up front, and the weed I would receive after the money got there. Calling Allison to give her the information, I had her send the money, keep a $100 for herself and buy me some gym shoes. She did everything but send the money to my guy. I didn't find this out for some time. Before this was revealed, I went on a mission with the crack. The five years I received at the parole board had woken me up! I was ready to fight for my life again.

The dorm had turned into a ghost town with all the crack that was in there. Inmates who smoked on the streets and thought they had it together, didn't. The homosexuals were turning guys out to smoking left and right. So many games were being played that it became like a project for real but only in close proximities. I jumped right in the middle and started making things happen for myself.

The crack got me some weed, and I took over another inmate's prison store plus sent money home. The crack put me in a good position prison wise to make the even $1,000 off the weed in cash only. This would make a $600 profit without counting the other money I would pull in.

Allison kept telling me she had sent the money, and I had my guy keep checking on his end, but there was still the $100 debt for the crack. My guy ended up going to the hole along with another inmate who owed me $150. Finally, Allison came clean about not sending the money. She had, in fact, spent it all, she says on the baby. I was still understanding about how hard it was for her and still trying to come home. This was her ideal, and she wasn't holding up her end of the bargain. I wasn't sending any more money her way. We had to try some other ways for her to help. In the meantime, the inmate who owed me the $150 got out of the hole and sent the money to the address I gave him. It was Allison's. Now I am trying to catch up with her to let her know not to spend it because I made another deal for the money. In the end, she spent this money also, and so I owed two dudes in the joint.

Allison is still coming to see me and write. The letters and visits are starting to be less anticipated as the realization of her decisions became real. Also in this I haven't told Lamar yet that all the money was gone. I end up going to the hole for fifteen days. After I got out, my main hustle became extortion; in the joint we call it *running a store*. I began to send money to another source. I am still trying to get out. On our last visit, Allison talked to me about a guy who had just gotten out of prison, and he left the girl he was with when he came home. She began to question me if I would do the same to her. She never understood I loved her but was not in love with her. For our daughter, I would have given anything to make it work.

August '98 was the last time she came to see me. For a couple months, she wasn't even writing. By December, things are heating up in the dorm again. Some of my brothers had tried to run a press game on another inmate. The inmate called his family to get them to send the money so he wouldn't get jumped on. My brothers came to me for a deal on some weed for the money. He never told me where the money was coming from or who was involved. I trusted my brother was head up. So I gave him an address to send the money, and this is how I got involved with this mess. On top of this, the sergeant's clerk ran a store also, and I was getting a lot of his business, so he pushed my name to the sergeant. Just before I was picked up for another investigation, I received a letter from Allison stating her and Lamar were coming to see me to talk about getting me out. I had spoken to Lamar about the money being gone and for him to not pay for the lawyer because the price I had to pay for being a sucka was to stay in the joint.

So now they had talked and would be down on December 26th. The first swoop of about eight guys came a week before the 26th, and the next swoop came two days later. I was in the second swoop, being held as the leader of an extortion ring. All the GDs in the dorm got placed in the hole with me being the main focus of the investigation. Allison and Lamar came to see me with my little girl on the 26th; it was a weekend, and there are no visits on the weekend while in the hole.

I began to say forget it and started giving orders to stock up on fruit and candy bars to fake a hunger strike. After fifteen days, we were all let out of the hole. While bringing my pack-up back to the block, the institution investigator was walking past and told me, "I thought I had you this time, Horace!"

I was out of the hole a day or two before being called to the sergeant's office to be told my grandfather had passed away. Two days later, the chaplain called for me to say, "Your father passed away." I was so bound up inside that I couldn't cry. I could only think of them dying, still thinking that their child is a thug, gangster, dope dealer, thief, addict, liar and many more. Calling my mom to support her, Allison and the baby were over there. This is how I found out officially that she was leaving me. Two days apart I lost my father and grandfather, on January 7th and 9th, then on the 10th, my girl tells me she is gone. I got to the breaking point; no longer do I desire to hustle or anything. I moved to the honor dorm and got out of the game. This may have been my toughest period in prison. Where I am grieving over the loss of my father, grandfather and the loss of a relationship that had been there so long.

Allison and I continued to talk on the phone, with me trying to get my $550 from her that she didn't send for the packages. She was trying to tell me who the dude was she left me for, but I wasn't trying to hear it because this wasn't the first time. She had had other relationships before; this wasn't that big of a deal to me. Finally, one day, she kept shooting it at me and I said, "OK, who is it?" To my surprise, it was the guy who had just gotten out and left the girl he was with during his time. I knew right then it was over because she had never told me she didn't know who to choose. I knew right then that I no longer had her heart. Now I'm cool with everything. All the lies and deceit is over with. I stopped calling and let things be even though it hurt bad. Because I won't hustle, I am taking a royal beating in prison. A guy I grew up with had come down and we became best boys. He would look out for me regularly, but he wasn't hustling. He was getting money from home. Scat was his name, and we shared a lot of things in common like we both are Capricorns, and we worked out together. We became support to each other because prison is hard on you mentally. Plus, we grew up together in the streets.

August of '99 things started to become better for me. The feelings passed some, and I was able to cope with the losses better. I get a letter, $100 bucks and a big stack of pictures from Lamar. The letter is saying how he let Allison come between us and he apologized for not being there for me the last couple months and to call him at this number because he is paying for the lawyer. I called the same day, and we called the lawyer on three-way. At

5:00 p.m. that evening, the lawyer was paid and gave a guarantee of my release.

I moved back to 8 house after the softball season; my team lost in the championship. The unit manager only moved me in the first place to play for his team. Being separated from this environment and these dudes had me not wanting to deal with most of them. Coming in from working out, a dude called my name asking me if I remembered him. Turns out he was a young dude who was in the streets a while ago, and he was best friends with Allison's new guy. We started kicking it, and before I knew it I was back smoking weed and hanging loose.

Rachel had started writing me. We began to try and have the relationship we never had. I was back talking to my two boys and planning to move in with them when I got out. While this is taking place, the guy Allison is dating comes to Orient too. Now this is hard for me, I am constantly reminded on a daily basis that I am a loser. Not only have I lost in life by being in prison, I lost someone who meant a lot to me, I lost the hope I could have a family, I lost the only person I thought cared about me. We are all in the same dorm, sleeping in the same sleeping area, right across from each other. At this point when all of them got there in the same dorm with me, I hated Allison. Now she is coming to see her guy and taking care of his business. Him and his guys were respected with everyone on the compound knowing my girl is with him.

'99 ended! We all managed to get along and lightweight got to know each other. It was hard to see him go out on the visit to see my ex and on top of this I couldn't see my baby girl. I had to stop calling and writing my baby because it was causing conflict. Allison and I had our last conversation agreeing to allow her relationship to become more secure. We both knew our daughter couldn't take any more drama. She needed not to see her mom changing men. My child needed stability even if it wasn't with me.

Waiting on my lawyer to handle his business, I was just lying around working out and discovering the gift God gave me. I've always been a leader in my workout crew. I had motivational skills and was creative with them. For all the years I worked out, I had never read a fitness magazine. I picked up my first *Flex* magazine in '99. I read the magazine from cover to cover several times. This is when I decided to become a personal trainer. As I kept reading the books, more stuff came to me. The institution didn't have a formal exercise class. I came up with the idea to write a proposal for an exercise class and submit it to the director of recreation. The problem was I had never written one and didn't know how. I began to use my influence with staff to get information on how to write a proposal. Finally, after receiving enough information on how to put it together, I did. Before submitting the proposal, I got some heavy supporters to back me.

The rec director took the proposal and told me he would get back to me. I had already been working for recreation in the weight room with a female officer as my boss. Soon my boss and I became more than inmate and officer; she became my girl.

Instead of the rec director giving the exercise class to me, he gave it to another inmate who soon messed up, and the director asked me to take over. Now I was waiting on my lawyer, running my exercise class, and having sex with a lady officer in prison.

My lady friend wanted a relationship when I got out, but I told her the truth that it wasn't going to happen. So she chose to mess with my homie instead.

Calling my lawyer one afternoon, he tells me not to miss the bus. Over the weekend, we party hard. By Sunday afternoon, everyone was just lying around. When Monday morning came, I was awoken by the guard letting me know it was time to roll. At this time, my incarceration was six and a half years, so I had accumulated a lot of stuff. I gave all my stuff away, said my goodbyes with my partner Scat walking me to intake. It took the sheriff a couple hours to get there.

As soon as I stepped on the van, I saw a homeboy I hadn't seen in at least eight years. On the ride back to the county jail, he was filling me in on the latest happenings in the city. He was also telling me about this female who worked at the county jail. She was a young girl but a hot one. Coming into familiar parts, my heart started beating faster with anticipation of finally getting through this nightmare. Arriving at the county was just like I remembered. Sitting in the waiting area to be logged in. The female who my homeboy spoke about was working the first floor. Homeboy pointed her out, and she was nice. The man called me to the desk to take down my information. As he was repeating my name, the female was near and overheard. As I was walking back to my seat, I could hear her ask about me to her fellow officer, questions like "What he here for?" She disappeared behind a partition and came back with three other female officers. Come to find out, this female was a little sister of a girl I used to date. The other two girls grew up with me. Sitting in the waiting area, I got a little bored and wanted to talk to someone. I started dialing numbers and made the biggest mistake to date. I called Allison to actually tell her myself I was coming home. And to tell my daughter. Never before had I been more sincere about not getting involved with her other than being a parent. The call was never accepted, I tried a couple more times but then gave up.

Being back in the county was like having the celebrity status I was accustomed to. Everybody was hollering at me and admiring my body strapped with tattoos. On the phone, I am talking to folks I hadn't talked to in years. The county had cable, so we watched videos on BET. I hadn't seen videos forever, so I am all into this. Every plan I had even becoming a personal trainer went out the door. I was ready to hit the streets again. The plan was to live with Rachel and the boys. She was already starting to lay stuff off on me. I hadn't seen Rachel since the day I got caught. The first time she came to see me, I was amazed at how she had grown. She looked so good and mature. The bronze skin with the hazel-colored eyes. Plus, she had always been slender but now had thickened up. But something was up; I couldn't quite place my finger on it.

My court date kept getting pushed back because my lawyer was in a murder trial. After a week and a half sitting down there, my lawyer comes to see me mad as hell. He goes on to say the judge called him going off about my calling Allison and threatening her and the baby. He goes on to say Allison spoke on how she would be scared for her life if I got out. I am sitting there listening in disbelief because I never talked to her, and the last time we did talk we said we would always love each other. All I could say was I didn't do it and explained who she was— the female who he was first dealing with him and had bailed out on me. The judge at this point wanted to send me straight back to prison without even seeing me, calling me a stupid ass. His comment was I brought him down here to let him out, and he goes and does this. In the end, the judge agreed to hear me out. Lamont wasn't protesting my release, so the prosecutor's whole argument was based around a couple fights in prison and this letter from Allison. The judge's decision was to send me back to prison. He stated he couldn't let me out and I hurt this woman. But he did agree to let me out if she would get in touch with him through my lawyer. Ever since January 1999, I had dropped to my knees in prayer calling on God to come back into my life. So returning to my cell, I began to pray and ask God why. How could a lie hold me? I shed a few tears because not only was I not getting out, but someone I cared about, someone I felt no matter what I would be there for them when needed, and lastly, my child's mother was responsible for taking this chance for freedom away from me. Not only did she write the letter, but she turned down the opportunity to retract her statements or meet us on any ground to get me out. This made me hate her with all I had. Her actions caused pain to me, my children, my family and friends. The crazy part to this is everyone believed I did what she said because of my past. Everyone who I told that this was a lie only believed her even more. With thirty months left to see the parole board again, I knew one thing. Wasn't nobody going to be in my corner. I was truly on my own.

The Return

I walked back to the dorm with my locker box trying to put my best smile in place. All my homies already knew I was coming back. On top of everything, I had given my stuff away, and now I had to rebuild. There were so many questions in my head. I just couldn't understand why this had happened. Now I'm back in the same dorm, in the same bed, looking at the same people. After believing I had cleared my biggest hurdles in life coming back to prison after almost getting out proved to be a greater one.

I was back maybe three hours before the first joint got smoked. When the weed kicked in, I just started thinking. I declined the next joints and meditated on my situation. In order to accept this, I needed a reason for why I was sitting back in this place. After sitting on my bed for some time the only reason I could come up with it was just not my time. My next order was to devise how I was going to take care of myself. Just so happened a guy who owed me three boxes of cigarettes before I left was out of the hole. Then I wrote my mother to send me a clothes and food box. Plus, she sent me a little money. Also to help me get things together was my buddy Fat Cat, who gave me a blanket and some items. Another homie gave me a box of cigarettes. It took me a couple of weeks to get situated, but when I did, my plan went into action. I started a store again.

This wasn't about my past goals. This wasn't about what I could do in the future. All this was about that prayer I had when I asked God to remove me from the situation and the life that I was living. And now I sit here with thirty more months remaining back to the parole board with the only hope of getting out of here is by getting my act together. And this is when I called on myself, I called on all the things I used to say about myself. I used to always tell people I was Superman. I always used to say I was thorough.

I then began to do my exercise classes again and got a tutor job in the school. Things begin to come together for me. I bought me some gym shoes and boots, got a new radio, and was able to keep my brand-new state clothes. All this time, I kept praying to God to bring me closer to him.

I didn't have a desire to make money and send it home. All I did was take care of my bodybuilding needs. I began to buy *Flex*, *Muscle Fitness*, *Men's Fitness*, and *Men's Health* from the library guy every month.

I came across fitness books that were sold to me. The vision and success of B.O.S.S. Fitness began to grow in my mind. Instead of just having the idea and settling for that, I began to write out proposals, programs, and business plans. By working in the school, it became easy to get one of the female teachers to give me advice on how to write these plans out. I started dealing with all the female unit managers and case managers on the compound. In exchange for information about how to write out these plans, I would give them exercise routines and nutrition plans.

My reputation for fitness began to grow among everyone. Inmates and staff began to seek me for advice and contribute to the vision. I had a partner who worked in the school with me. He caught a dirty urine and had to lay it down for a minute. His job was the guidance counselor clerk with his own office and computer. By him being gone, the position was open for me. The problem was I couldn't type, and I had never been on a computer. But I'm a fast learner. That was my pitch.

I got the job and ended up teaching myself how to type and how to work on a computer. At this time, I made the goal of doing something toward my future every day. Also at this time, I started getting involved in institutional programs, only the ones ran by the women. The system in Orient among those who played the girl game was like a tight-knit circle. Once you were in, you couldn't fight nature. Men and women were made to be attracted to one another. Once a person came up once, the circle would talk. If you could keep your mouth shut, you were sure to come up again. The first time a person comes up, it's automatically double platinum. In order to reach platinum again, you had to get sex and money. A gold album was when you like each other, and she would feed you and play the game, but not go all the way. At this time, I had reached double platinum and a stack of gold albums.

I'm keeping weed but not as a weed man this time but as a businessman. I didn't concentrate on nothing on the streets. Everything I was about was in the joint with me. I had a new friend with whom I spent time with from Monday through Friday. Three days throughout the week, I would go and see some other prospects. On Saturday, I would go and spend time with another female who was feeling me.

All these women were in the rehabilitation part of this. They didn't wear uniforms. We would talk more about what i was going to do when i got out of prison instead of what was going on in prison. I got so caught up in prison that I was buying brand new state blues every week. Now I had six pairs of shoes with at least twelve outfits. The pants tailored to fit a certain pair of shoes or a certain style.

I never wore a washed pair of state blues but would give them to the youngsters after my laundry man washed them. There was an oatmeal man, a fruit man, a sandwich man, muffin man. I literally didn't do anything but call shots. My oil collections had gotten so big, I had one bag made to hold them. Then I hooked up with another homie who was doing his thing and we started getting money with a football ticket. I'm at work from 7:30 a.m. to 5:00 p.m., and then I go work out from six to eight, come back, take a shower, fix something to eat and I'm ready to do it again.

There was a CO who worked on our pod on a regular basis who was a personal trainer. All along I felt dude was the real police, but he had keys to the things I wanted, fitness information. He also began to try and get next to me like he was with the rest of the dudes. He would sell me fitness food, but he also was so caught up in the prison that he began to do the things we were doing. Small beefs began to take place between us.

Everything was still going on around me. There were guys who would come and talk to me about how they couldn't handle being in the same situation as I was with my ex. There were guys who made jokes about it, and guys who tried to use it to their advantage. Those were the times when Allison would come and see her dude, and it would bother me.

This was especially after we got into a fistfight. So the talk became that he took my girl and kicked my ass. I had to always remind myself that I was doing everything now because I wanted to become a better person, a better father and become a success in life, It was hard! Over time things started becoming easier and less stressful. Her guy and I became cool, not friends. We started to have each other's back, break bread with each other and we took a stand on not allowing outsiders to influence our thoughts.

I knew the things I was doing weren't real, so when I would have downtime, the truth would come. So I stayed on the go, doing things that kept the pain away. When I first got to prison, the first tattoo I got was Allison's nickname across my heart. Even through this mess, the tattoo still remains across my heart. The reason it's there is because it represents some very significant places of my life. It no longer means I love her or want her, but it keeps me reminded of how things could be.

In many ways, I was still holding on to her because my feelings toward her were the motivating factors to a lot of the things I was doing. When the spirit of depression hit me behind still being in jail, I studied fitness harder or created a new plan. I had to find some positive outputs to this negative situation. I was making up my mind to really become somebody. I was tired of being labeled a thug, etc. I wanted people to look at me and associate me with something good. I've always been a smart person with a good sense of humor, very quick on my feet, plus I have a creative side.

I'm a loyal, dedicated person. I just had all the energy that could present these good qualities channeled to being a gangster who does good deeds. I was still smoking weed and cigarettes but wouldn't drink the wine. The women I was dealing with believed I was one of the good ones who could actually turn his life around. They began to pour things into me I never thought about. The plan was birthed to get paroled to a halfway house in Columbus. Columbus is the Mecca for fitness in Ohio, so I was going to make it.

Even without knowing when I was getting out, I still believed that I would make a statement in the fitness world. My portfolio began to get bigger, and I continued to write out these plans and write the vision of the type of building I wanted. A lot of people began to even call me B.O.S.S. Fitness. I know they were making fun of me. Since nobody really could see themselves capturing their own dream, they joked about mine.

I would tell anyone who would listen to my dream to become one of the best trainers in Ohio. The same look came across everyone's face, the look of doubt. When I came back from court, an older dude out of Columbus named Slim became my closest confidant. He was very smart and observant. He began to have my back, no matter what. He would never try to play for none of my stuff, and he would hold me accountable for my actions. Slim became like a big brother to me. He watched me go through a really hard part of my life.

The bitterness, jealousy, envy, strife, pain, all these things were taking hold of me, and I was spiraling out of control. The police were breathing down my throat tough. The sergeant pulled up on me asking the last time I had some sex. My actions had made a lot of dudes envious, jealous, plus mad at me. Here it was. I was jealous of Allison for moving on with her life and looking happy, and these fools were jealous of me because I got some cigarettes, food, state blues, shoes, and a couple hundred dollars. They were looking at these women in my face like they were something.

Ain't no real woman going to play herself out on no job with someone they could never really know. The male COs were either trying to suck information out of me or salty because the female wouldn't holler at them. It got crazy. I started to argue with COs plus fallout with dudes because of what I'm doing. Within a year of me being back from court, all this happened. Since what goes up must come down, some drama had to come. Because of my position at work and the type of weight I carried around the joint, staff members took it personally.

And the way I walked around like I was untouchable, a staff member elbowed me in the chest and told me to get somewhere. He goes on to tell me I ain't nothing but an inmate. He asked me what I was going to do about it and he said he would lock me up so tight my head would spin. And as I looked at it, my head wasn't big. I wasn't being cocky. I was actually being confident, and I was starting to see myself as more than a loser. And since I was seeing myself differently, others were seeing me differently, too, and that was the challenge.

There wasn't no jealousy, there wasn't no envy. It was these individuals seeing somebody that was taking strides toward bettering themselves, and they knew seriousness when they saw it. So rolling on past this episode, I continue to work on my future and play with the women. A central office guy came in to check out how the school was being run. He wanted to know all the clerks' positions and everyone with access to a computer. My job was terminated inside that office, but I continued in the school.

One morning the police rode down on me to have me piss in the cup. Dirty urine. I knew it was over. It takes time for the test to come back and even more time for the sergeant hearing and the push to the Rules Infraction Board (RIB). I turned all my attention on getting my money right before I went down. I had a lady friend I'd fallen out with once because she began to get jealous of some things. By her being twenty years older, she was schooling me. But I was so out there, I was missing what she was really saying and doing. I made a move that was risky but costly. Either way, I made a move on my buddy's friend who was digging me anyway. I broke my cardinal rule, which was not to write any letters just pop from the hit. I wrote the letter, and my friend found out. The next thing you know, I'm in cuffs going to the hole.

Because I was smart enough to mention things we had talked about in the letter, she took a risk of making this move. My day in court came with old girl coming down and protecting both of us. So I took all the way out like I was supposed to receive more time in the hole. I just laid it down, waited on my dirty urine ticket to surface.

Once it did, I got additional time on top of the time I was doing. While in the hole, I started thinking about how I had been acting and the things that were going down. I had a lot of fun, but none of this stuff was worth risking my freedom. Sitting with eighteen months to go to the parole board, I needed more focus. I continued to study fitness and write plans. Even from the hole, I was able to help staff members in their training. My partner Lamar was making sure things were straight for me and I was receiving messages from the same woman who placed me in the hole.

The hole shot was a true reality check. One I needed badly. Even though I wasn't thinking about selling drugs on the streets and carrying guns, I had some character flaws that could hurt me in the long run. I was still in touch with God and still searching for change. The one conclusion I came to while in the hole was play time was over with. After doing seventy-five days for the letter incident, I began to do time for the dirty urine. Back in the block, the whole dorm had received a piss test.

This resulted in something like a hundred dudes who came back, and they need a space for them. Everyone on LC that had dirties got out before completing their time. Since we all had dirties, we had to go to the mandatory yellow jumpsuit drug program. We're still on the compound, but we have to wear yellow jumpsuits, go to the chow together and are not allowed a radio, food, shorts, etc. Plus, when we go outside, we can't cross the yellow line. This made me feel even more like a sucker. The only good thing about being in this program, my ex-girl from the weight room was a regular CO in the pod now.

So we kicked it a little. After doing sixty days in the jumpsuit program, I was finally back in the block. This was September 2001. I wanted to stop hustling, but was scared to be without stuff. My partner Lamar kept my store running while I was gone, so immediately I started putting things together. My first month out, I made $500 on store moves only. I wouldn't mess with the weed or smoke any.

By December 2001, the word around the compound was the prison was closing. We had been hearing this for some time, so no one believed it. The first move the administration made was to close our block down and spread us throughout the institution. I was moved to 3 house along with my partner Slim.

The regular CO over there was a female. This was the kind of female a man could really fall for. She was tall, good looking, and had class with long hair. She and I became cool through another CO when she first started working there. My thoughts were the same about getting involved with these females. Before the 8 house boys came to this pod, there wasn't nothing going on, so we decided to put some life in this spot. I began to gamble again but stopped running my store. Around Christmastime, the weed hit the camp super strong.

I was still maintaining my restriction from weed, but I soon broke down. The smoking began for Christmas and went on nonstop until New Year's. The first of the year brought the first ride out to make the shutdown of this prison real. This only made the prison become wide open. The CO'sdidn't know what would happen to them. So they stopped caring about a lot of stuff. Everywhere you went, dudes were blazing weed. Even some of the CO's started smoking weed with us. From the moment I moved over to 3 house, the female CO had been doing some extra talking to me.

It seemed like every time I would come out of the shower, she would do a round. She liked to work out and was looking good with it, so this became a topic between us. She had a habit of yelling at dudes. I was at the microwave heating up my food, but she had called count time. Not hearing her call it, she began to yell at me. This really upset me because there wasn't no need for that. After count, I went to the desk to basically check her about raising her voice at me.

She took it well, but the next day she stopped me and told me she respected me for bringing my feelings to her, and she added how she really wanted to flip. This conversation turned into an hour-long talk. From this point, we would talk a little more each day. After a couple of weeks, we had a pretty decent rapport. I was going to the microwave to heat up my food for the NFL playoff game. When I went past the desk, girlie was sitting there with something heavy on her mind. The line was long, so I went to the desk to kick it a bit until my turn came.

We began to talk and before we both knew it, a couple of hours had passed. We both agreed to eat and for me to come back after I got finished. So I came back, and we talked until count time. After the 9:00 count, there's only about a half an hour left before she leaves, so we talked for that also. Now this is becoming regular for us to talk at least four of the eight hours she's at work. I was already a dorm porter, so she switched me from first shift to her shift and had me work in a day room around her.

I could tell things were progressing between us, but my trust wasn't there. So I kept downplaying it. Talking one night, she asked me, could I be friends with a female without having sex with her? After we finished this small talk, she began to say she wished I was getting out soon. This freaked me out. So I told her she wasn't my type. She was playing it also because she told me her sister would be nice for me. We began to trade secrets about our lives with each other. She would tell me something, and I would tell her something.

She had told me a deep secret that only her family and ex-boyfriend knew about. She then began to try to get me to match this secret. I really couldn't match the secret or wasn't willing to give this much of myself to this woman. As the guys came back from chow, a dude told me my ex was working in the weight room. So when they called recreation, I slid past girly and went down to the weight room. When I got down there, my ex told me she knew I was coming. The end result is we had sex and told each other a bunch of lies.

When I got back to the pod, it was a couple of hours later. Girly got to asking me where I've been. I began to lie to her where I had been. Then she started in on me about telling her a secret. Finally, I told her that I just got finished having sex. She was shook at first and didn't believe me. I wouldn't tell her where I had been or who I was with. I just said I had sex. She still wanted me to tell her something, so I said, I like you. She wasn't ready for that but accepted it. Her question began with, why did I say she wasn't my type?

I started laying it all on the line about the hole and my trust issues. She sucked it all in, and we began a relationship that night. For the first time in a long time, I felt like a man. She made me feel special. The way she treated me, looked at me, and wanted to take care of me. We spent every minute we could together talking and enjoying each other. The old CO from 8 house was coming around. They had worked out together a few times. She began to challenge his information with what I was giving.

Before 8 house closed down, he came to me about him getting his own studio place called B.O.S.S. Fitness. He would be working with the more mature generation.

Another female CO who was cool with girly and myself would come and hang out with us. She had been at the gym with dude also. So when I asked him about his gym, they both wanted to know.

This caused friction again between dude and I. Another shouting and challenging match began with my homeboy having to get in the middle. Girly was the type of woman I was looking for. She was twenty-nine with no kids. She was in school for a medical profession. The first kiss between us was like we had been doing this forever. She was bringing me bodybuilding food, chicken breasts, turkey breasts. We both knew I would be leaving to ride out soon, so she worked overtime in the block to spend as much time with me as she could.

The second bus Load had rode out to North Central where I was going. Because dudes had been getting caught with weed on the other rides, the institution began to piss test guys straight off the bus. This still didn't stop me from smoking. I thought there was a way to beat the test and I could do it. Girly found out I was smoking weed and got mad at me. Because of her upbringing, she had never messed with a dude like me. She couldn't see how a person who was already locked up could hurt themselves by smoking weed in jail.

We were talking about being together when I got out and this posed a problem. Finally, my papers came, and I'd be leaving in the morning. Our last night together was special, but sad. We shared a good kiss and held hands, looking into each other's eyes deeply. The last words we spoke was she would write as soon as she started her new job not with the state.

North Central

My last night in Orient was monumental because this meant a new opportunity for me. This was another chance for me to change my ways and get my life on track. We woke at 2:30 in the morning to begin this forty-man move from institution to institution. Everybody was wondering how it would be coming to a new place. We were coming from a prison where just about everything goes, so we really didn't know what to expect. Upon our arrival at NCCI, the first thing to take place was to be led two at a time to the piss bottle. Even knowing this was coming I still took the risk and gambled again with my life. The previous busloads sent word to what was happening and again I failed another test. The staff and the inmates wanted to remind us, "This wasn't Orient. These folks actually thought we were coming in to try and run something, Orient boys this, Orient boys that."

Myself, I'm thinking, "These boys need to grab a hold of life."

The COs and inmates were overly protective of the women and on guard for anything. Every time I looked up, someone was looking at me. The culture change was a trip. My beginning days were hard as far as sleep and adjusting to the way prison life was run here. A part of your survival tactics behind these gates and walls are sounds, the mood of the place and understanding who is who and what is what. It took about two weeks to get adjusted. Before I could get the lay of the land, I was picked up and led to the hole for my dirty urine. From the hole, I registered for the voluntary six-month drug program. I also signed up for four other programs. This was my way of being a smart man.

170

I liked the old cliché, a smart man will think himself out of a situation; a wise man will not get himself into. This being my second dirty urine within eight months plus having that letter-writing incident, I knew the parole board would give me at least six more months. I accepted this fact and prepared myself to handle things to come. I continued to pray every day, and I really got stronger mentally while in the hole.

I wanted to stop smoking cigarettes and weed. I wanted to stop hustling. After all that I had done in my life, I realized I hadn't done nothing. To this point, I hadn't managed to hold a job on the streets or in prison for more than a year. For all the player stuff and trickery, I was sitting in the hole looking forward to doing more time because I couldn't control my addictions.

I got out of the hole on April 8th, 2002. This made forty-five days exactly.. I started my first program two days after getting out of the hole (SMART Choices). Something inspired me to want to stop cussing. Because of my goal to become a personal fitness trainer, it became essential to me that I look the part through and through. My speech needed to be automatically arranged without cuss words or slang.

When September rolled around and the six-month drug program started, this is how I actually learned what my addiction was. Even knowing I had one, didn't mean I understood my addiction. I knew nothing about triggers, addictive behaviors, addictive personalities, none of these things that caused a person to relapse or start messing with drugs.

In the first phase in the program, one of the classes is a twelve-step video with a guy named Alex Johnson. He is a recovering addict who has decided to take his message to other addicts. In one of the videos, he asked us to think about what we think about the most. After a pause, and then, "Do you have it?" He stated that this is your higher power. For me, this time it was fitness. Because one of my many prayers had been to get to know God better, this revelation that God was not truly my higher power sent me in search of Him.

With the perspective of wanting to get to know God better, I started going to Sunday morning church services. In the eight-plus years of my incarceration, I have only been to the chapel three times. Once for a service because my homeboy asked me to roll with him. Another time to get some free Christmas cards, and the other one was when they told me my father had passed away.

This first Sunday, I said that Jesus Christ is my Lord and Savior, and every week I would go to the morning service and afternoon service trying to receive a word. I began to study the word. Up until this point, I thought my actions were in check. I thought because I didn't smoke, drink, cuss, that this meant something. Come to find out, I had a whole lot of work to do.

In order to graduate from the drug class, I had to attend sixty meetings. While attending these meetings, I became a co-chairman of the Tuesday morning NA meeting. In this role, I was able to understand from another addict's eyes the effects the lifestyle was having on myself and my family. My addiction exceeded the drugs. It was an obsessive need to feel loved.

With this new understanding of what addiction was and how I came to depend on mind-altering substances, my life was becoming actually more complicated. Now, I want to know how a little boy who loved his mother and protected his family turned out to be this monster capable of committing heinous acts of criminal intent repeatedly. Trying to live with myself was part of the reason I depended on people, places, and things to fill me on the inside. I had feelings of betrayal, neglect, underachievement, irresponsibility, loneliness, so I remained in the spirit of fear, false evidence appearing real.

While I was finding God and in the drug program, those who knew me well began cracking jokes on me, but it didn't matter anymore. While the same dudes were still going to the hole, fighting, smoking weed, etc, I was in church, in meetings, doing programs and facing my inner demons.

Things were starting to happen to me that had never happened before. My popularity and respect were a shock to me because I didn't have any money, drugs, or the gang life. People started depending on me to give them inspiration. I heard things about me that I could never dream of being said. I have charisma, humility, talent, gifts; I was a person who actually has something to say.

Even with these good things going, I still had to face the music for my past behavior. At the parole board, I was given twelve more months for the dirty urine and everything else. I still continued to seek God and do the best I could at maximizing the current state I was in. Hearing a preacher speak about calling your future and letting people know who you are from your situation. This made me draw up a letter and send it out through the cities of Dayton and Columbus, letting them know who I was, and I will be coming soon to make my mark in the fitness industry. Before the drug program ended, I enrolled in college. Now, I'm in college for the first time. I'm in a classroom for the first time in at least sixteen years. My goal became to do something I had never done, which was make all As. The first quarter, I missed getting As in every class. The next quarter, I bore down hard. I came up with the dean's list, all As. Making the dean's list gave me more confidence.

Knowing you are smart and actually getting a result from it, is totally different.

In the end, two quarters had been completed, and it's time to see the parole board again. This time, I was referred to a parole board panel because of the nature of my crime. This was December, and I had to wait for the decision.

Now, the school is finished for the moment, and a parole board is behind me. I sat down to reflect on the past two years of my life. My daughter Toby had been visiting me with her grandfather for the past several months. My visits with her opened a lot of feelings that I didn't know existed. See, back in the drug program when I was working the steps, some serious revelations occured. Step five was to admit to God, to ourselves, and to another human being the exact nature of our wrongs. At this point alone, I looked at myself and really accepted who I was; even knowing I had done all the things I had done, never meant I had accepted the responsibility for the things. I believed *others* made me do the things I had done. Back in '93 in the county jail, myself and a couple of dudes jumped on this guy real bad. After this, I hadn't seen that guy but one time until getting to North Central.

I didn't even remember what he looked like or his name, but he never forgot me all these years. We walked around this place for months waiting on the other to make the wrong move. The key was we both had changed but had not been faced with the ghost of the past. So it was difficult. After working step five, this made me go straight to this man and ask for forgiveness, and I understood if he wouldn't grant that to me.

In step six, I was entirely ready to have God remove all these defects of character. The thing about character defects is, I only found them out by having this adversity in my life. My obvious flaws were easy to identify. This was hard work. Seven, I humbly

174

asked him to remove my shortcomings, give me the inner peace to really let that guy go. (The old me) Eight was a hard step because it was too long, so I had to start with the people fresh on my mind. I made a list of the persons I had harmed and became willing to make amends to them all.

At this step, Allison came back to my mind because now, I can see the direct result from my madness. This was a good girl who poured her all into a worthless person, only to turn herself into the person she can love, which meant she no longer could love me. I wrote to her, telling her how I realized the mistakes which were made and began to ask for forgiveness.

Working the 12 steps helped me in so many ways. The steps made me look at myself first, look at my role in my life, with my addictions and the pain I caused to myself and others. I reflected back on how I found out my best friend and brother, Lamar, had gotten killed. It was a letter from my little girl Toby consoling me about the loss.

Lamar and I hadn't spoken to one another since December 2001. He came to see me to let me know he was upset with me for threatening Allison and preventing myself from getting out. What I didn't understand and neither did he, I didn't do it and neither did she, it was bigger than all of us. But, In my stubbornness, I stopped talking to everyone because they wouldn't or couldn't believe me when I said, "I didn't do it."

Now, here's another person close to me who died while I was in prison, and died still believing I was this horrible character. The tears I shed for him were real, and a picture of him still remains in my Bible to this day. I will miss him, and in my prayers, I ask for recovery for his family. I hope he is looking down on me with a smile on his face because his partner is making it out.

In the past two years, I've been tested in so many ways, with me passing most and failing quite a bit. The one which comes to mind was when this fellow convict became aggressive with me over something. He had been picking on me already, so it was bound to come to an end. He stepped to me, and I shocked everybody because they had never seen me angry. Only the grace of God could keep me from going all the way. That crazy look and that sound in my voice matched the way I was thinking. When the dude sat down and shut it up, it allowed me to walk away, going to get my workout gear to work some steam off. This dude made a move to put his shoes on and go sit back down with his homies. This almost sent me through the roof. Going to the gym and working off some steam, I came back and walked straight up to dude and apologized for my actions.

He played me like a cold sucker. This sent a rage in me that lasted for several days. I literally had to keep praying and talking to God because I wanted dealings with this dude. Finally, after several days of listening to Fred Hammond, I anointed myself, the tears came down, and at this point, I began to ask for forgiveness again. I also learned that I had a long way to go on my walk. Overall looking back, I could smile at the trial and tribulation because I can see success in my life. My dreams had become more of a reality with each waking moment.

With a positive attitude, you can do anything, but there are still more things for me to learn. My past had not been completely released by me.

At the parole board, the parole lady made a comment about my daughter's grandmother. My daughter's grandmother had written a letter to the parole board that was not in my favor. This really tore me up because I had just received a five-page letter from Allison asking me to forgive her and her actions.

This made me reflect on how the letter was written to keep me in jail back in 2000. Now, they wrote another letter to keep me in jail again, but this time, the attempt didn't work. Having to find ways to remain positive and to find understanding. Because I have changed, doesn't mean others changed. It also doesn't make others believe you have changed. I had to remind myself I was still in prison. Because of the mother and grandmother, I told my daughter I would be leaving prison in February 2004 to go to a program which would not allow me to contact anyone until April. April was actually my release date. To this day, I can't figure out why I did this. Sometimes, my best thinking still yields weak results.

So for months, I had no contact with the one person who has stuck by me through all of this. My entire ten years of incarceration, she never ran in and out of my life, and she always wrote words for her Pops. My plan for April 2nd was to call her once I got to the halfway house in Columbus. I still wasn't planning on going back to Dayton until I got my feet grounded.

When April 2nd came, I was still sitting in prison waiting to get out. From there, my date moved to April 12th, but yet I was still sitting in prison. I had felt bad because I lied to my daughter. This made me sit down and write my daughter along with her mom to explain the whole situation. Just like before, no answer. I continued doing things to stay busy and not lose my focus. Nothing really could quench the thirst and hunger inside of me, but the opportunity to live life. This same opportunity I took for myself was now being held in the hands of people who don't care if I succeed. This made my desire and drive come alive even more because in order to really live life to the fullest without short-changing myself, I had to battle the odds.

Here, I am planning my steps one by one without knowing when, where, or how to get them accomplished. By May 5th, which was my next follow-up date, I was still sitting in prison. By now, I am just going with the flow and trusting God. We can have all kinds of plans, but in the end, God has his plan. Each of us is a unique piece to a much bigger puzzle. We never know whose life we're going to affect. All the greatness within me is still going to be revealed through fitness. The road to getting there has definitely been changed, altered, and very much disrupted, but the one thing I do know is no road will be too tough, and nothing will stand in my way to achieving the ultimate goal, which is to make it out of that damn life.

The next struggle for my release day came to be May 28th, 2004. The change in all of this is going to Columbus seems to be out because my parole officer is in Dayton with the state just releasing me without nowhere to go. Basically, I'm being put out of the institution. Upon hearing this, the first thing that happened was fear and anxiety. I'm feeling like, "How are you going to put me out of here to do this by myself? I don't take care of myself well in this type of situation. All I know is to manipulate people, use drugs, guns, and women."

For thirty minutes, I went through this. In the end, I began to be grateful and praised God. First thing, I am a new creation. Second, when I was a child, I spoke as a child, but now I have to concede that he didn't bring me this far to leave me. I am not going to overthink my situation, just trust in me as always. I have the ability to make the right choices. I know what's good for me, and what's not. Even if I get into a rough spot, there's something greater in me than he that is in the world. I have one direction to go in. Anything that doesn't feel right isn't the same direction.

PART III:

Turning My Life Around

My Release

The final Days in North Central were hard. Having to stay in prison two months longer than my original out date was challenging. Not being able to get out because I didn't have a place to stay was hard because it meant nobody was in my corner. I can tell you it only motivated me more. I was ready to put my plan to action. The day my name was finally called was surreal. Like you dream about this moment for so long and now your name is being called. When a person leaves a place like prison, you leave behind folks you have become close to due to your circumstances. Everyone is always happy when someone makes it out, and there are always some who are sad that you are leaving. After many handshakes and words of encouragement, my close comrades and I shed a tear. In my mind, there was supposed to be someone waiting to pick me up, take me out to eat, and family friends waiting for me at the house to celebrate. That was my mind. The truth was that what was waiting for me was a state-issued sweat suit, a check for $95, a pair of state-issued boots, and a van ride to the bus station. After ten long years, nobody was even at the door to hug me. On top of this, I have $95 bucks in my pocket to start my new life, and with all this, I was still excited about putting my plan into action.

Prior to my release, there was a two-year span where I didn't hear from any person on the street. Not a letter, phone call, or visit. Somehow I missed the folks I loved, but whenever I was feeling low, I would just work on my plan and continue to envision myself being successful. I believed my success could bring my family back together. When I had a moment to be down about anything, I would pull out my study material and work on my plan. In my mind, I believed that I was so much of the problem and that I had let so many folks down that I had caused this separation between myself and the outside world by going through what I had to go through to become who I was. Becoming a man in jail made my change only privileged to those who have been a witness to it. For the outside world, as far as they know, I am still the same person that left the streets. Because I was ready to take responsibility for my actions, it never crossed my mind that the same folks I was trying to prove my change to weren't supporting me during one of the most difficult situations any person could go through.

So I was at the bus station ready to get started. After placing my belongings in a locker, I began my mission. When I had about a year until my parole board hearing, I wrote a letter to every gym or studio in Columbus explaining who I was and my current situation. In the letter, I spoke about my passion for fitness and my thirst for knowledge. I asked if anyone could be so kind as to send me any fitness-related information. Once I got my parole, I wrote to the same companies again with a different letter. I spoke directly about my intention to become one of the top five personal trainers in Ohio. How I was willing to start at the bottom as the janitor. I also said in this letter that I was on my way. So when I got to the bus station, my plan was to put in an application at all the gyms I had sent letters to in downtown Columbus. I stopped first at a fruit stand and purchased a fruit tray for $12. That left me with $83 of the $95. Completing my tour of the gyms and putting in applications, I took a walk through the Civic Center Mall. You would have no idea of the changes in ten years. It looked like a scene out of *The Jetsons*. Everyone was on a cell phone! After a few hours of enjoying freedom, I called the halfway house coordinator to pick me up.

During my last two years of prison, I had gotten involved with heavy programming and finding peace with God. Attending religious services two to three times a week and fulfilling my AA/NA programs requirements of two meetings a week, I was in a good place mentally. One of the volunteer groups from religious services was going far and beyond for us guys in there. Having someone who just cared was huge, and these folks spent their own money, gave their own personal time, and really supported us guys. The group also started a halfway house called independent living. The program was six months with your first month being free, and then you have to pay a percentage of your income after. Their goal was to help with clothing, jobs, and transportation. The group would volunteer their personal time and money to come and share their insights, beliefs, and encouragement with us.

So, When he arrived to get me, my excitement got even bigger. My journey was on its way! After taking me to get some chicken, I was dropped off at the halfway house, and I remember thinking, This is it. Like a few hours ago, I was in prison and now I am sitting on a couch with guys I was in prison with looking stupid. Not having too many folks to call in jail didn't leave a ton to call out of jail. I surfed through my phone book for someone to call but couldn't reach anyone. After a few hours of this, the moment came. The phone rang, and another coordinator tells me I have to be in Dayton to see my parole officer first thing in the morning. The coordinator picked me up to make a 6:30 p.m. Greyhound bus. There was a young lady in the car with her. I really couldn't see her face, but I could hear her voice. Being straight out of prison, I was craving a female touch. I needed a female attitude, I needed female interaction. This young lady, Mika, ran several halfway houses herself and was really into taking care and supporting men coming out of prison.

Riding in the back, listening to the sweet sounds of female laughter was soothing until I saw that McDonald's sign and had to get it. I went in to purchase a meal and gave the young lady my money. In return, she gave me my change. Something was totally wrong. The bills were correct, but the coins were fake. I went back to the van holding the coins in my hand and had a funny look on my face. The director asked me what was wrong, and I said, "She cheated me. The young lady gave me tokens instead of quarters."

The director looked and started smiling and said, "Those are the new quarters."

I had been in prison so long that the money had even changed.

I got to the Dayton Greyhound station still not knowing who to call and where I was going to stay. I called Scat, who had been home for a couple years. He answered the phone and couldn't believe I was home. Scat picked me up. Took me to his house, gave me a couch for the night, and some clothes to put on. The next morning Scat had to be at work, so he dropped me off in downtown Dayton an hour before the parole office opened. After buying a pair of tennis shoes, I headed to see my parole officer. I had to sign some release papers to have my parole switched to Columbus. My parole officer gave me five days to stay in Dayton to reconnect with family.

Leaving the parole office, I had nowhere to go. So I did what I knew. I got on the bus and headed back to the hood. Getting to my usual stop from years ago, I started walking around Westwood in disbelief. So much had changed. The neighborhood looked run down. The only place I knew to go was over Bryant's. Knocking on the door, some guy I didn't know answered the door. He must have been new because he didn't know who Horace G. was. I began to walk back around the hood checking out how things just didn't look the same. The man at the door was Bryant's mom's husband. When I left, he called his wife and asked who I was. Bryant's mom called him and before you knew it Shoop was full of everybody, celebrating my homecoming. The homies started pulling me aside to update me on the happenings and who was snitching and who broke and who got it. Everyone was asking me what I was going to do.

When a person gets out of prison after such a long time, their success, their story will be written on a split-second decision. Right in front of me is the game, the life that I loved so much, the opportunity to get right back in and hold it down. My homies were looking for Horace G. and got James. I began to tell everyone about my plan to do fitness, stay in Columbus, and never come back. The same homies who didn't write, send money, or pick me up at the door began to offer me drugs and money. I was offered a car, a place to stay and a pack to get back on my feet. In this split second, I made a decision to get away from them and back to Columbus I went. BTW, my homies gave me thirty days in Columbus and I would be back living in Dayton.

So the first thirty days were for my homies. The second thirty became about me. After twelve days of being out of prison, I landed a job. Remember when I applied for those gyms after getting straight out of prison? One of the gyms gave me an interview. I went down there so confident. I was interviewed by two managers who looked at my prison-issued resume and started laughing in my face. Both managers took pleasure in my situation for a few more moments before letting me know I could not get the job. Leaving the gym, I noticed a young man cleaning up. I asked the young man to hook me up with a job. He informed me he worked for a cleaning company and the guy who runs it is Gabe. I asked for the number and left. I continued to ride the bus around a town I have never been in. Going from gym to gym putting in applications and calling daily to check on them. On my twelfth day out, I was frustrated and needed a job because I had no money. Sitting at the table calling gyms, I noticed the number for Gabe. So I called, and he answered. I told him who I was and how I had just gotten home from prison and needed a job. Gabe told me if I could get to Best Buy at Easton Town Center, I could get a job. Gabe said get there and call him. Needless to say, I got to Best Buy, called Gabe, and he gave me a job. Not only did Gabe give me a job, he bought me some work pants and got me lunch and money to ride the bus back to the halfway house.

Now during my job search, the coordinators did their best to help me as much as they could. The program was new and everything they wanted to do wasn't in place. So we were really on our own. I had done ten years, another guy had done three years but was used to going back and forth, and the other occupant had done twenty-one. It was crazy because we were finally out of prison, and we didn't know anything about survival in the real world. On top of this, the program couldn't offer any help.

I started my janitor job, which was a split shift of four hours a piece. 9:00 a.m. to 1:00 p.m. and 9:00 p.m. to 1:00 a.m. To get forty hours, I had to do this. The job paid me $8 per hour. I was so happy to be earning money. I only made $20 per month in prison. Eight bucks didn't sound bad to me at all. I went to work every day with energy and confidence. My plan was to start at the bottom, and I was doing it. Learning how to clean up a gym to me was just as important as owning one.

The program didn't provide food for us, so I had to be wise with the little money I had. Spending thirty dollars every two weeks at the store, I purchased tuna, noodles, beans, and I would get an oven pizza and chicken nuggets for a treat. My first adversity came after my first check from working. The coordinator first started asking me for money to stay there. Second, she started demanding gas money for the rides I was given. Third, the house phone got cut off. To make matters worse, the water went, and next came the electric. Here I am out of prison only thirty days, and this is what I am facing.

As hard as it was for me to be sitting in the dark, not having water to use and no way to contact anyone, I still went to work on time. I cleaned that gym like it was mine. I began to build relationships with the members. Because of my finances, I sometimes didn't have bus money, so I walked and ran the three plus miles to work. Since the bus didn't run at the time I would get off work, I would run home also.

During this time, I started training folks for a ride to work or a ride home. The lost and found box was my home. I would get clothes, water bottles, CD players. I never took anything because I was stealing. I didn't have anything, so I was getting things out of the box that I needed. One evening while cleaning up, I saw four women on the treadmills. I heard this voice, and I knew this voice. I couldn't remember from where, but it was familiar. Then I saw the face and the smile and was instantly in love. It was Mika from the first day out!

Progress

Mika and I began to date. At the house, things had gotten worse. We received a message that if someone comes to the door, don't answer it. Turns out the house they were using didn't have the ok from the owner. We were being thrown out. I made a call to an old friend of mine (Rochelle). I explained to her my situation, and she said she could help. She volunteered to come up to Columbus and take me around to find an apartment. I had only received one check from working at the time, so I didn't have much money. Rochelle offered me $500 to help me get a place. I found a place which had a one bedroom for a price I could afford. I talked with the manager and explained my situation and that I had nowhere to go. He gave me a chance and allowed me to get the apartment in my name with no credit, and he waived some fees so I could afford the upfront payment. After getting my electric turned on and getting a small phone, I was flat broke with a place to stay.

The apartment was on the bottom floor of the building. I chose the bottom floor because it reminded me of the hole in prison. The first thing I did when I got the keys was lay spread out on the floor and cry because I finally had my own place. Not having any furniture or dishes, clothes, food, the basics, still didn't deter me. I was winning. Before leaving prison, I had scripted what I wanted my first six months to look like. It went like this: First month to find a job. The second month to find my own place and get my driver's license. The third month was to get a second job and open a bank account. In the fourth month, get certified as a personal trainer. My fifth month, I wanted to continue to save my money.

The sixth and last month, I wanted to be working part time as a trainer.

Mika gave me a bed, a small table, and an alarm clock as a move-in gift. We continued to see each other, and things got serious fast. Mika was the first woman I had spent real time with in a decade. I had been so lonely intimately for so long. I believed I was in love in a month. Mika took me to her church and introduced me to all eight of the members. We both were trying not to have sex until we got married, so we kissed and touched a lot. We would spend everyday together. Meanwhile, I ran into a homeboy Wayne from the city. He and his family opened their door to me for dinner and conversation. Also living in Columbus was a homeboy Marcus who had his own church here in Columbus. Wayne and Marcus would pick me up, take me out to shoot pool, and chill. Marcus would pick me up for church and just be a friend also.

After being in my apartment for a couple weeks, I hadn't received another paycheck from my job. Gabe kept telling me to be patient and gave me a story. Gabe gave me one of his work trucks to drive around and to get back and forth to work. I considered this a consolation prize for not receiving another paycheck. I continued to go to work and do my job with integrity. Never late and never slacking. I would be pushing a trash can with bags on my waist and a sweeper on my back. A member would stop me and ask me to spot them. I had started to become popular like I worked for the gym and not as a janitor. Becoming really cool with the staff of the gym. Talking to one of the young men named Ben. I spoke about not getting paid for working and that I needed to find a job to pay the rent. Ben mentioned his father works at JCPenney as a manager. He said he would talk to his dad about this. The next day Ben told me his father said go fill out the application online and then let him know when I did. He would pull it for me.

Within one week I got an interview and was hired. I was hired on to the top position in the warehouse. Usually someone has to have experience or time in to bid on these positions. Here I am getting hired for it, and I am receiving training to be certified as a forklift driver. Now I am working JCPenney's morning shift from 5:00 a.m. to 2:00 p.m. And doing the janitor job 9:00 p.m. to 1:00 a.m.

By the time my rent was due for the first time, I was late. I still had not received my check from the janitor job, and it took three weeks to get paid the first time from the warehouse job. I received that check and had to give it all to the rent man. I was struggling, but I was out of jail. One evening after hanging out with Wayne and his family, he drove me home and came into my apartment. Wayne had never been in; I always just came out. When he walked in, his eyes got big. I only had a bed, a table, and a clock. My homeboy was hurt about this. The next day, he showed up with a couch from his den at home. A couple weeks later, while hanging out at Marcus's office, we were laughing and joking and he asked me about a TV show. I told him I didn't have a TV at home. Marcus, without hesitation, gave me the TV in his office.

Nobody could understand how come I was so happy and excited. When I would clean the door windows in the front of the gym, it would take me forever. I would open and hold the door for everyone coming and going. I spoke to everyone and walked like I wasn't a janitor. I had folks laugh at me and say smart shit about me being down on my knees scraping gum off the floor. Nobody understood I was free after ten years. I have a plan to be dominant. I have a plan to take care of my family. We want second base. I had to learn how to survive as a free man, but I never changed the plan. Let's go!

While training Mika and her friends one evening after management was gone, I turned around to see the head personal trainer watching me train this group. He walked away, and I finished up. Because I am not supposed to be doing this, I thought I was going to lose my job. Coming from the back room, Bill was waiting for me.

He said to me, "James, you are not a janitor."

I was like, "Huh?"

Bill said, "You are a trainer."

I told Bill my dream to become one. Bill tried to get me hired as a trainer, but it didn't work out. What Bill did for me was get me a discount on my personal trainer certification. I didn't have the money, so Mika paid for my packet as an investment into my career.

I worked both jobs, worked out, and studied for my test. At the warehouse we worked on production. Your pay rate and your level were judged on how many pieces or how much weight you can move consistently over a six-week period. I never missed a pay upgrade period. Once I hit level six, I just had to maintain it. I was making $15 an hour. I had started to buy clothes and necessities plus save money. During my breaks at work, I stayed at my station and studied. Before heading to the gym to work out, and then do my four hours, I would study. Finally, I completed my studies, took the test, and passed. I am a certified personal trainer.

It's Working!

While continuing to work at JCPenney and working the evenings at the gym, I would rent a car to drive to Dayton on the weekends I didn't have to work overtime. My relationship with Mika had ended, so I didn't really know what to do with myself when I did have free time, so I went to Dayton to connect with my kids, see old friends, and catch up with family. The one thing I noticed was everybody had their own lives that didn't include me. Another common theme was most hadn't grown in the ten years I was gone. Folks were still living the same way.

My goal was to save $2,000, get ten clients, and leave my job. Now I had been able to furnish my apartment with the necessities and then some. I have money in the bank, feeling like it's working. In need of two things for the plan to work was a place to train and clients.

I found a newly opened gym called Christian Fitness Center. I went in looking for a job and walked out signed up to be an independent personal trainer. Agreeing to pay $250 a month for lease fee. Using the money from my job to pay the fee for the first few months.

While working as the janitor, I saw this guy Sam being trained by one of the trainers there and saw no progress. I approached Sam several times, offering him three free sessions to try me out. After several times, Sam agreed to try me out. Sam became my first client! Gaining a few more, I met Marcus. He was working out at the gym I am training at. We began a training relationship with Marcus being my fifth client ever.

Pulling up to the gym one evening to train, I saw this lady on the treadmill and she was freakin' fly. At this point, I hadn't been moved like this since being home. She was about four-feet-eleven, brown, pretty skin, big smile, and I mean big smile. Her body was tight, and she looked young. Come to find out her name was Debbie, and she was a radio personality on the local radio. Debbie thought I was hot also, so we began to talk and spend a lot of time together. Needless to say here I go again. (She's the one)!

My training business was picking up. I had twelve to fifteen clients, $2,000 in the bank and was feeling really good. JCPenney had hit its slow period. So managers began to look for folks who would take a volunteer lay off for a month. I jumped at the chance to see if I could make it as a trainer. After the first month, I wasn't ready to go back. Things were going good. So I asked for another month. After the second month, I went back to JCPenney. The first night now on third shift. I was wheeled out and taken to the ER. Turns out I had a panic attack. The next morning, I woke up and quit my job. Now I am a full-time personal trainer.

Right after quitting my job, the owner of the gym came to me and said he was making some changes. In order for me to continue to train out of his facility, I had to have my business registered with the state. He gave me thirty days to have this done. My certificate came on the thirtieth day. From this point, the challenges started coming. First, the gym owner kicked me out of his gym for cussing. Next, I lost seven of the twelve clients I had. I had upgraded my car and now had a car payment, rent, food, phone, and electric. Within two months, my savings were gone, and I was only making enough to pay my car, my phone, and rent.

Debbie held me down during these hard times. She would feed me daily while I was racking up overdraft fees on my bank account and my credit cards. Riding one evening with Debbie, we drove past this locally owned gym. It was closed, but I was able to look in the window. I went back the next day to talk to the owner. I went in asking for the independent trainer opportunity. His fee was $500, so I accepted and took the next step to reaching my goal.

At Dream Fitness, this guy was a beast. He had a different style, a different approach to fitness. I started there in July 2005. I had five clients with no money and in debt. I then ordered a Dell computer so I could create flyers to pass out. The computer was at 27 percent interest. I began to make and print twenty-five flyers a day that had to be passed out before I got home in the evening. In between clients at the gym I would be there all day soaking up the game from Dale, the owner of the gym. I would stand outside in front of the gym and wave at everyone driving by or walking by.

Things were starting to get really hard financially. It got to the point that I called my old boss at JCPenney and asked for my job back. He said that he didn't have my job, but he had a second shift head deliverer position and would give this to me. This meant no more lifting heavy boxes or standing in a cold or warm trailer unloading. I would be just moving palettes when they are ready with a forklift and managing others. I needed to go back out there and fill out a new application and call my boss to let him know so he could pull it. An interview was set up for two weeks later.

During my two-week wait, Dale and the other trainers went out of town and left me to hold the gym down by myself. New customers came in, old ones switched trainers and next thing I knew, I was so busy training the day my interview was supposed to take place that I missed it. By the end of September 2005, I had made my first $5,000 as a trainer.

1079 N. High

$5,000 per month turned into $10,000 per month. I was meeting all kinds of people from different backgrounds and ideals. My life in Columbus is really starting to take form. I was doing the one thing I prayed for (workout for a living). And now I had folks paying me for it. My plan was going according to schedule. With the money coming in I was able to pay off the debt I had accrued during the struggle months, paid off my car, I was paying extra on my rear child support and keeping up with my current. I was beginning to save all the money I made the fourth week of every month. If $3,000 came in that week, I saved it. If only $200 came in, I saved it.

By the end 2006, I had saved almost $40,000, moved into a brand-new apartment with new furniture, and I had been out of the country for the first time. I was crossing things off my bucket list like going to see all my professional teams play live. Let me tell you, I was enjoying life. I was starting to feel normal, productive; ultimately I was proving to myself that I wasn't a loser.

When things were hitting their stride for me, Dale informed me that the gym would be moving, first into a temporary space and then into a much larger space. The agreement we made in the beginning was about me serving his vision and then we both working together. So, even during the transition into the temp place, I continued to support him. Meanwhile, I still had to maintain my client list, which was about forty people. The temp place wasn't a third of the original Dream Fitness and all the equipment couldn't fit in. It also was very challenging to keep everyone motivated.

In order to keep my folks happy, I started training them at their homes, parks, and at other gyms. During one of our meetings Dale mentioned that he was changing the plan when the new space opens up. Instead of one of the rooms being called B.O.S.S. Fitness, I needed to turn my client list over to him and he was going to take a higher percentage and cut me a check every two weeks. Shocked about the change, I started thinking about getting my own space now, which would move up my timeline and change the plan some. Looking at a space here and there and frequently meeting with Dale to see if he was really going to break our agreement.

Mrs. Sara was one of my clients who had been with me about a year or so. Mrs. Sara is a really good person. She is about helping folks and making things happen. She was one of the few individuals I shared my past with. I have to say my story didn't run her off; instead she wanted to help me more. During the gym moves and tension between Dale and me, everyone could see the stress on me but also the dedication and loyalty. So when Mrs. Sara talked to me about an opportunity she had for me, her spill was how she had seen me be loyal to Dale from day one and also how she had seen how when the energy changed I didn't.

Mrs. Sara showed me a space she had a lease on and was willing to sublease to me for a portion of the rent. Before we could make this happen, I had to meet with the owner of the building for him to agree to a sublease. At the meeting, I presented Mitch the owner with a proposal about my business and how I was going to use the space. Just like that, I had my own space. Mrs. Sara gave me such a great opportunity. The original rent was $6,000 per month in a prime location with parking and 3,800 square feet. Mrs. Sara also gave me a jumpstart with the rent, which was $1,000 for six months, $1,250 for the next six months and $1,500 for the remaining six. After eighteen months, I had to pick up the full

$6,000. She added in a bunch of office equipment, a desk and chairs, quality stuff.

After the last meeting with Dale to get him to change his mind, I began to work on getting my studio opened. I would train all day from gym to gym, park to park and house to house, also with my free time I would be working on the new studio painting, cleaning, etc. I went to the bank to apply for a loan, but I didn't have the credit to receive one. What I did have was my business certificate for being in business for two years. For this I was given a credit card with a $9,000 limit.

I began to look for equipment and found this company in Tennessee. The crunch was on because I had rent starting in my new place on April 1st and a lease payment due to Dale on April 1st. So after finding the company and meeting my rep over the phone, we set up a day for me to drive down to the factory to pick out my equipment. I was on the go so hard at the time with training my clients all day, working on the new studio, and stressed about this thing working. My meeting was in Tennessee on a Saturday. I had to train all day on Friday and got home at my usual 8:00 p.m. I went straight to bed so I could wake up at 1:00 a.m. to hit the road, so I could be at the factory at the designated time.

Heading to pick my equipment was an awesome feeling, so awesome that I made it about two hours out before pulling over to a Wendy's to take a power nap. I was driving by myself drinking Red Bull trying to stay awake and the drive took a few more hours more than usual because I was pulling over frequently to sleep, get out the car, and walk. Honestly, this was sheer willpower, making it on time to make my purchase. The crazy thing about this is I had to jump straight back on the highway because I had training sessions the next morning.

By the time the doors opened April 1st 2007. I had run up the credit cards total $9,000, spent the $40,000 I had saved, and with only $1,400 in my bank account, business began.

The transition went smoothly, with most of my equipment on the way. I began to train my clients in the new space with body weight exercises and the use of dumbbells, calisthenics, and agility movements. The arrival of equipment was a monumental moment for me. I had this feeling like I was on my way.

After being open for a few short months, Debbie calls and tells me that one of her coworkers is looking to get in shape and start a Fitness Club. She gave him my info, and we connected. Big Man was one of the morning hosts of the top hip hop radio station in the region with over 100,000 listeners daily. He wanted to not only get himself in shape, he also wanted to help others get in shape.

The way we started the Fit Club was by making me the fitness expert for Columbus. We went on air introducing me and my company and opened the registration with emailing Konan and he would pick the participants. The response was so overwhelming that we had to cut off the registration. Every week I went on the radio to do fit tips and to talk about the fun things we were doing with the fit club. Konan and I helped change a lot of lives with our efforts. Our program shaved hundreds of pounds off our group. There was Ben who lost over one hundred and Tammy who lost close to one hundred and many more who lost ten to twenty pounds.

We were using our talents and skills to help others. The fit club was free to the participants. After the first group of members, it was time to open registration again, and it went through the roof again. We ended up with two groups. I was running the Fit Club and training my current clients and trying to build my business. This would leave me with getting to the gym at 5:00 a.m. and not leaving until 8:00 or 9:00 p.m. I was working on the weekends as well. In order to get some rest, I would fall asleep on the chairs in the front of the gym. I would sleep there so I could hear someone coming in.

After eighteen months of being in business, The Fit Club had been a success. I had been able to fill up the gym with equipment and hire trainers to help with my vision. Things were rolling along, and at this point, I still hadn't taken out a loan. The fact is, I had paid off the credit card bill and the lease loan for the equipment I took out to get the doors open. The bonus was getting my back child support paid up, and now my credit score was starting to climb.

Living

At this point, I began to work harder than I have ever worked before. I also began to take advantage of the opportunities that were out there. Moving into an upscale apartment, purchasing a brand-new Cadillac 2009 in 2008, I was still saving money every chance I got. One of my clients had shared with me a savings technique that was very helpful. She instructed me to automatically have $50 per week going into a savings account. $200 per month! She also told me to never have an emergency big enough to dip into the money. She also worked with me on how to start saving for retirement by not going on the trip I had planned for my birthday. As the money started coming in, I spent it right back on the business but never missed a savings moment.

During my time while things were going so well, I was busy being honored with an Entrepreneur of the Year award and numerous newspaper articles. I was asked to speak for various organizations. Literally with all that was going on professionally, my personal life was coming together as well. I had welcomed into the world my first grandson, Damon. I spent every moment I could with him. I was at the hospital the first night he was born. Every two weeks after that I saw him for a day or a weekend. My grandson was my guy. The gym was thriving but not without challenges. Trainers come and go; that's the nature of the business. It was the owner of the building, Mitch, who was becoming a challenge.

He would call me on various moments and cuss me out or talk to me like I was nothing. I was one of the first black-owned businesses in the area, so there were challenges that came with that. I was called a cavalier because my goals were bigger than their actions. When Mitch called, I would just suck it up because of the goal. When the other owners would treat me like I was nothing, the goal was bigger. I was fighting for something great and didn't have the energy to feed anything else. During 2008 when the stock market crashed, I was in the gym watching CNN listening to everyone's take on what to do. There were tons of interviews, but only one caught my ear. The young man being interviewed said this was the time to get in the market, not run away from it. This began my journey into purchasing my own stocks. I went down to the bank, set up a broker account, and bought my first stocks. I would go down to the bank when I had free time and talk to the man who helped me set up my account, and he would give me tips. After six months, I had doubled my first investment.

Since one of my goals was to be a mentor to men, the trainers that came into my business I treated like they were brothers. I began to embrace them with something other than a job. Things such as motivation, I would take them on vacations, buy them gym shoes and make sure they could make as much money as they could. It was common for me not to charge a trainer a percentage for six months in most cases one year. It never made sense to me that I was the only one eating. The biggest gift I gave to my young trainers were customers to train. B.O.S.S. Fitness was making its mark in the fitness industry.

Our customer base ranges from fourteen-year-old athletes up to sixty-five-year-olds who just want to stay moving. We had a kids' fitness program for three- to five-year-olds and we did travel fitness. We like to call our fitness program Average Joe because we wanted every person to have a strong fitness level without the pressure of trying to look like a fitness model. Our customers travel, they have fun, they eat out, and they have tons of work functions. So finding a way to reach their goals with their busy lifestyles made us open up to flex training. This is where you could train at a time that was good for you, and if your schedule changed, we could accommodate it. We accomplished this by training multiple folks at the same time while still having individual attention working your program. This gave us the ability to make more money in less time and still get folks to reach their goals. One of the best things I have seen come out of B.O.S.S. is our clients started becoming friends and hanging out with each other outside the gym. My staff came over to my house. We laughed together, we mourned together, and we climbed together. With this motivation I made the switch from calling my customers clients to members. To me, it meant you were a member of a family, not just a dollar sign.

B.O.S.S. Fitness was thriving on a major scale. So good that it made things difficult when Mitch called one day and told me I had thirty days to get out of his building. He had this call because after the sublease of eighteen months, he placed me on a month-to-month agreement. At this time we are working on being in this space for five years. At $6,000 per month, never late and always paid before the date, there was something about my plan that I started noticing: I had a timeline, but the force of nature had one also. I was always pushed to move before my time. I didn't want to rent again, but with Mitch breathing down on me again, I was over it. I began looking for another space and found one. The location I thought was perfect for what we do, and it didn't take the current members too far out of their routine.

There were two problems with the new location. First parking was a mess, and second the owners of the space wanted me to put $60,000 upfront with the rent being higher than what we have. Still on a crunch to beat the thirty days, Mitch calls me and tells me I can stay. I wasn't about to stay; it just bought me more time to figure things out. When I received the deal from the new space's owners, I sent it out to two of my current members: Ted Dobbins who is a really phenomenal accountant, great with numbers, and makes awesome business decisions, and Derrick Smoke, who is a lawyer with a real estate business and makes deals all day for a living. Both came back with Are you a damn fool? This is a bad deal; you can buy something for $60,000 down.

So I turned down the opportunity to rent the new space and started the mission with Ted and Derrick to get a new space.

333 E. Livingston

After weeks of looking for a space to purchase, things were not going so well. Derrick and I were running into a ton of resistance from realtors and space owners concerned whether we had the money. While we were looking for the space, I was getting ahead of the financing by applying at several banks. I was getting turned down left and right. Bankers would agree to meet, see me walk in, and the look became so common I knew that a no would follow.

I got one meeting at a local Columbus, Ohio, bank based on my financials being great and my personal credit. The one thing they couldn't see from the financials is that I was a bald, short, muscular black man. When I got to the bank and told the young lady who I was, she asked me to sit down and I waited for one hour. The next thing that happened was crazy. I was escorted into the meeting by two white men and sat down in between them with another white guy standing up and another white guy behind the desk. The way I was talked to was to this date the most racist moment I had ever had in my life. The whole scene was something only in the movies. Without a doubt I was told no on the loan right there, handed my financials, and escorted to the door. I went to my truck and cried so hard. I was in a position where I met the requirements. I did all the work I was supposed to do. I pay all my bills, I have the money and the business, and my skin color was the only reason I couldn't get the loan. I had to stop and ask God if I was doing the right thing here. When your option is to sit and take it, be humble, and don't end up in jail, your dream has to be bigger than their actions.

After getting myself together and going back to the gym to finish work. The pressure was starting to mount. I am now responsible for other folks. My guys have families and need to put food on the table. No matter what was happening, I still managed to not cheat the members of the energy they loved about B.O.S.S. I gave them everything I could. I kept applying and kept getting turned down. Reaching out to another banker who worked at a bank I had prior relations with. I got a couple loans and paid them back before the time, again my financials are great, my credit score and the score that the bank creates for us was great. When he came back to me, it was with a big fat no. The letter that was sent said I lied on a current application and that they no longer wanted to do business with me. This prompted the banker to put his job at risk by bringing me a copy of the said document, which clearly showed I never lied. With tears in his eyes, he apologized for this and stated, "I really wanted you to get this."

Right after the meeting with the banker, I had to meet up with Derrick. He found a building he thought was perfect for me. When I got to the space, I was already defeated. The building smelled horrible, had no windows, a big tree in front, the parking lot was busted up and I couldn't find financing. After sharing with Derrick my experience with the banks and I was giving up and renting the other space, Derrick began to tell me a story about his cousin, who now has the largest African American construction company in Ohio and maybe the United States. He shared how his cousin came to Columbus and was turned down by over 20 banks before being told yes by one, Derrick told me we can put windows in, we can remove the tree, and we can get the smell out. His speech was so motivating that I left there with a new energy.

The next day talking with Ted About the bank controversy, he said that he would talk to someone for me. Ted's contact was the owner of a small community bank named Heartland Bank in Columbus, Ohio. The contact he had was with the owner, Shane McDaniel. Through email we were introduced, and Shane asked me to send my financials. I remember thinking here we go again. After a week went by, the committee had turned me down. I informed Ted of the situation, and the next thing I know, Shane wanted to meet me at the location. Shane and I talked for a while. I let all my emotions out about what I had been through with the other banks, what I had to overcome in life to be here, and how I had mouths depending on me to provide. I told Shane if he would take a chance on me, he wouldn't regret it.

Shane looked me in the eye and told me, "I am giving you the loan. I am your partner. If you have any problems, just call me." Now the building is sitting right in the heart of new construction, free standing with parking. This was not my will but a source with greater power. I did the work from never missing an appointment, taking care of my family, being honest when no one was looking. My upbringing made me strong enough to get back up when I was being knocked down and now I own a building for my business, which created another business, a part of the goal—B.O.S.S. Realty!

The challenges of getting my building ready for operation were there. I was working again at the current space during the day and at the new space during the evening. I served as my own general contractor even though I was supposed to have hired one. I had made up my mind that I wasn't paying Mitch another $6,000 so at the end of the month I moved all my equipment into the new space while we were getting it ready, shut down my business for a month and went to work. I was sleeping two hours a night, if that. My stress level was at an all-time high. I managed to put it all on the line again. This time things were different than five years earlier when I didn't have as many responsibilities. To only have $20,000 left to run my business and my personal life was stressing me hard. I had never bought a building before; I had never renovated a building before. Only four months earlier, I had purchased my first home and got married two weeks before that. I had my grandson, my biological children, and now I have four stepchildren, and I still have employees who have responsibilities. We got that building ready in forty-five days and was slanging fitness in forty-six. Note: the second day of opening I ended up in the E.R. Again with a panic attack. Second note: Mitch found out I was gone by driving by the space to get his check and found it empty. He did call me talking strong, but this time I was ready. I cussed him out for thirteen minutes straight. Called him every name I could and went all the way up as close to a threat as you could go. Before I hung up, I told him we will see each other again but on different terms.

Growth

From opening day, the business started taking off. Purchasing the building was the best investment yet. I began to put away $10,000 per month. I wasn't the only person making money because the better the business did, the more I hired others to give them a chance. After about eighteen months or so into 333, we had an opportunity to do a corporate fitness program. The company had 200 employees and a fitness room in their basement. I was brought in to do a twelve-week weight loss program that had a twist to it. From the twelve-week program, it turned into several $50,000 contracts, expanding and remodeling their fitness room, and because of the presence of B.O.S.S. Fitness, the company's overall health numbers improved so much that the company received huge checks back from their insurance carrier.

At this point, the money was coming and so had the folks who started to give me advice as to how I should approach my business. See, the end of the twenty-one-year plan has me becoming a motivational speaker, sharing my story to help those who believe they don't have a shot. My goal is not to be a fifty-year-old personal trainer working in the gym all day, every day with no end in sight. So while the money was coming in, I began to do the next phase of the game. If first you must learn how to make money, then second you have to learn how to save it. After saving it you have to learn what to do with it, and forth learn how it can work for you. I was sitting on hundreds of thousands of cash dollars. The first thing I did was increase my stock investments to $17,500 per year. Then I started taking the profit from real estate investments and buying stock in a personal account. Before I knew it, I was saving in various ways 33 percent of my personal income and saving $4,200 per month in the business savings account.

Before I knew it, I was getting checks coming in so fast that I would lose one or two for a few months in pants pockets. The thing that I prided myself on was to continue to do the work. I didn't do it for the money as much as I had to accomplish something so I could get folks to listen to me when I tell you, you can do it. Just believe in yourself, love yourself, and keep positive energy.

I for sure needed to get my family to second base. My family was going to get the opportunity to chase their dreams just like I did, but they were not going to have to struggle like I did. We are going to have the things we need to get it done. I can't do the work for them, but I can give them a start to getting to the work.

B.O.S.S. Fitness has created several businesses in the Columbus area. I have mentored, inspired, motivated, and represented a measuring stick for many inspiring personal trainers to start their own business. These young men and women are impacting the lives of others, whether it be through fitness or employment. For me, I knew I didn't need much to survive. I had been through the most difficult times of all in my life. I was ready to mentor men. I wanted my children to count on me. I wanted to motivate others. The money is the bonus; the money gets people's attention.

My passion, my drive, and my work ethic had been the driving force to be of service to so many. B.O.S.S. is a place folks can come to for energy, for motivation and have someone they know care about them as a person. There is a trust factor attached to B.O.S.S. And it isn't for everyone. If you don't like hard work, don't come over here. If you don't like to be pushed, then don't come over here. I had to fight, pick myself up, motivate myself, sacrifice, hurt. Did you know I started my trainer career wearing a size 9, and now

I wear a size 11? I have had surgery on my feet, I literally gave everything I could to others and this was my dream, this was my why! Nobody understood why I worked so hard, they didn't understand I had a goal and it wasn't just talk to me. I did what I did so my sons could see a man work hard to make it. I worked hard as a trainer, as a business owner, and as an investor so my sons could see someone they know, someone they could relate to be successful.

After driving my business from the prison cell to now at the point of being in business for over fifteen years. I am proud to say I have logged over 175,680 hours of training, been personally involved in over 1,500 personal training members, performed over eighteen million steps, made over $2 million in sales, and have helped others open up their own businesses. I have become a great father to my children, a great husband, and a great protector and provider. The thing I am most proud of is becoming a great man.

Kay G.

One of my dreams when I was in prison, of course, was to find a woman. Saying "woman" has a different meaning now thanks to my wife, Kay. I remember the first time I saw her. She walked into the gym like she owned the place. She walked past me like I wasn't there. I remember thinking, I'ma' get that!

There was something about her that was different. After being out a while, I had gone through the "this is the one phase." Went there a few times! Haha. Then I got through that, and I went for the just having fun phase. Yes, I had lots of fun! And then there was the phase where I was not trying to get serious, but I didn't want to just have fun. I was looking for the girl who to her I was the man. I knew I needed to prove this to any woman, plus maybe living up to this standard myself. Because my woman had to be my woman, I for sure had to be her MAN.

My wife and I began our courtship very unconventionally. We became friends! We met at a time in our lives where both of us were looking for something different. I honestly know for a fact neither of us knew what that was. How else could you explain how this black man fresh out of prison with this crazy dream to become a millionaire meets this white woman from an upper-class upbringing with four children and a husband fell in love with one another.

It started with getting to know one another and having the stamina to continue to meet each other's needs. I needed someone who would make me feel like I was THE Man and she was looking for someone with direction outside the normal life she knew. Being friends first allowed us to work on ourselves and gravitate to each other's weaknesses. Back at Dream Fitness I was single, working from 5:00 a.m. to 8:00 p.m. most days. A home-cooked meal was welcome in my life. I would go out to my car at the end of the day and find a pan of lasagna in there. In the beginning, I wouldn't eat it because I didn't know where it came from. Then one night, the lasagna was smelling good, and I went after it! It was little things like that I needed, and Kay's instinct allowed her to bring them into my life.

The year we spent getting to know each other without sex, without the vision of being together but actually allowing a natural course to happen, developed with a simple friendship. She was able to knock down those walls and allow me to just be myself with her. I can tell you this, in the beginning we would talk and not know what the hell each other was saying. This is how different we were!

When I was first faced with getting my own space and the troubles at Dream Fitness. She was the first person I talked to. She told me that she believed in me and that I could do it. Her support helped me become comfortable with the task in front of me and gave me the strength to go for it. While I was in 1079 N. High all day sleeping on the chairs in the front so I wouldn't miss a customer. It was Kay who came down and sat with me when things were slow. It was she who brought me lunch every day. It was Kay who found out things or knew things I didn't know about running a business. She taught me how to dress in a way that kept my swag but didn't have folks afraid to approach me because my pants were on the ground.

The thing that made her so easy to flow with was she was just cool. When my grandson was born, she embraced him like he was hers. She would come over and help me take care of him. And let me tell you something, Lil Damonloves him some Kay. We together built B.O.S.S. Fitness. When business was picking up, but the money didn't say the same, she bought the needed treadmill. When I needed to go to the doctor on my break, she would drive me so I could take a power nap.

The most impactful thing she brought to my life was how to love. Kay and her family embraced me. Skylar and Duke, her youngest children, lived with us; they grew up with me. I never knew what it was like to actually be loved by your children until them. I believed dysfunction was the way it went. I believed you argued, yelled, and name-called. That is what I thought a father was to do. Sky and Duke made me feel like I was a dad, and this helped me change the way I treated my children and how I allowed my children to treat me.

Kay was the first woman I have ever been in a relationship with. This is why I asked her to marry me. She said to me was I sure? Ha ha ha! We got married January 19th, 2012, in Jamaica. Two weeks after coming back from our wedding, we bought our first place together. This made me a homeowner for the first time. Productive people produce, and our lives have been very fruitful. She has allowed me to focus squarely on my dream while she made life easy for me. We made one agreement to each other, which is a deal breaker for both of us. You take care of me, and I take care of you. That is both of our number one jobs. We are not Bonny and Clyde, Jay and Bee; we are James and Kay, two people whose natural gifts fit like a glove and allow us to be productive, successful, and loving.

The Twenty-One-Year Plan

I came up with the number of twenty-one years because the goals I wanted to accomplish needed to happen by my fiftieth birthday. At the time of my start, I was twenty-nine. Standing on that locker box reading that fitness magazine visualizing a life of success couldn't prepare me for all the people who would come into my life to assist my dreams. I never would have reached this point by myself.

My first Thanksgiving alone in Columbus, two of my members Mrs. Lucy and Michelle Smoke cooked me a whole Thanksgiving meal. A young lady named Bre' took the time to show me how I should be treated. Dale gave me the opportunity to be at Dream Fitness. The first person who gave me a chance to be a trainer was Rod, the owner of the first gym I was at. My boy Bill who helped me get a certification, and Mika who paid for it. Every step of the way, there was someone giving me information. Mrs. Sara with her assistant. Not only did she give me the opportunity to own my business, she remained a member purchasing 20 packs.

I have had trainers who came and supported my dream by giving me what they could to build B.O.S.S. into a place they could make money at. My family supported me by not harassing me about not making the family dinner. My children didn't get upset when I couldn't make every game. My wife took care of the house and made sure I had a comfortable place to come home to every night.

See, when you are chasing a dream and going all in, you will have to ignore many things. I learned a long time ago that you can't serve two masters. I couldn't build a business and win the father of the year award. I couldn't lead men to become men without sacrificing the things I wanted to do over the things I needed to do. Everyone around me made sure I could be in the position to be successful.

Having one focus for so long, tunnel vision is needed. Not going out to dinner on a weekday, always being tired, being totally selfish because what you did made others better. Members appreciated how hard I was working and took time out of their busy schedules to mentor me, like Randy McDouglas who stuck with me from Dream Fitness, to High Street and all the way up to my retirement. Then there is Branden Jacks, who doesn't mind sharing his expert views on how to make money. Nina, Shi-Town, Dotty, these women stood with me as sounding boards while I figured out who I was. At my most challenging moment in my journey, it wasn't about money, my marriage wasn't struggling, my children were doing fine, it was me struggling because I had lost my way. The awesome support system around me held me strong until I could take control of things.

Goals are good and I believe we all should have them. We must be very aware of not giving energy to those things and people who are not in our corner or the things that don't go our way. When we lose our focus, we take everything that has been good for us and take it or them for granted.

Twenty-one long years of fighting takes a lot. Hard is hard, and any goal is hard. Don't run from the challenges. When it gets hard, you get harder. When you take a loss, embrace it. When you have a victory, enjoy it. The key is when anything comes your way to keep your eyes on the prize. Getting overly happy or overly sad won't cut it. Trying to get there too fast will cause impatience. This journey was twenty-one years. Be motivated to do your thing, not do someone else's.

From my journey, I want you to feel excited about you. I want you to get motivated to do your thing. I want my energy to get inside your bones and have you doing something toward your goal daily. I want you to say, This guy wouldn't lay down and neither should I. I took the bullets, so you didn't have to. My path was a clearing room for others, even you. Just believe in your dreams, don't compare your dream or your route with another's. Information is the key; once you have the information, use it to be successful. I was told I needed to work three times as hard as the white guy. Shit, I just worked as hard as I could, and then worked some more and some more. I worked so hard I never got a chance to see how hard the white guy had to work. To me, again, hard is hard, so what difference does it make? It only makes a difference when you start looking at others' success and compare it to yours.

The twenty-one-year plan was just that, a plan. If you don't have a plan, don't look for results from a plan. You must decide to give you the best version of you. Success doesn't feel like success; this is when you know you are successful. Work hard, believe in yourself, and don't be afraid to have success.

My Children

When I went away to prison at twenty-four years old, my oldest child was five. The pride I had to be a father was there, but my ability to be a father was not. I didn't have a clue. I was nineteen when I found out Damon existed. The joy I felt when learning this news was one of the best feelings I had ever had. Jumping headfirst into the situation, I never sat back and wondered why his mom hadn't shared with me that we had a child.

The craziest thing about this is while getting to know Damon, I ended up spending the night with him and his mom one evening. She and I had sex again, and just like that, another child. So, we have had sex twice and came up with two kids. Boys at that.

My third son, Jamie, was also conceived from a one-time-only sex act.

It was a crazy time for me with my sons. Here was Damon at six months old when I found out about him. Jamie looks just like me, like a twin, and he was named after another man, and I had to sneak to see him because of his mother's situation. And my mom had to tell me Dre' was mine. At the time, I was living pretty good and had things figured out. I had the ability to help with clothes and shoes. I didn't see Jamie as much, but I've always had the opportunity to spend time with and take care of Damon and Dre'. They definitely were my guys, Dre' more so than Damon. Damon was a grandma's boy and never wanted to go with us. He just wanted to be up under her. Dre', on the other hand, we used to hit the town. We would get our hair cut at the same, he would spend weeks with me. When I was couch-surfing, my son would be right there with me.

When it came to Jalen, the female version of me, we don't get along for nothing in the world. We are so much alike that we both can go forever mad at the other. It is always easier to say, "I am not dealing with that" because we never have dealt with each other. Being my first daughter, and being so much like me, I have always thought about how things could have been. From the time she was little, her mother, April, created challenges to keep my Jalen and me from having a real relationship. At six months old, she up and took Jalen to Kansas. Even after coming back, her mom consistently moved, and I would have to find them. So once I went away to prison, I lost contact with my child up until I was about to come home from prison. The challenge got harder when her mom moved Jalen to Dallas when I was in prison.

When April went away to Kansas, it gave Allison and me time to get close. By the time I went to Kansas to bring April and Jalen back home, it wasn't to be a family but to have my daughter back.

By the time Toby was born, my life had finally hit rock bottom. My addiction was going strong, and my ability to hold things together wasn't there. Toby is my only child that was conceived from a relationship. Her mother and I fought to hold our family together as much as we could. The challenge for Toby and me was I didn't have a place to live, and I was not allowed at her grandparents' home. I was left to see her when I could. While Allison was pregnant with our daughter, I made another mistake.

Going to see Jalen one-night, April and I had sex. We hadn't been intimate in a very long time, and this was something that just happened. From this mishap, April got pregnant. So it was kind of a one-time thing. April ended up pregnant with twins. It wasn't until an argument with Allison that I found out the babies were still alive. When I approached April about this, she told me the girls were with her aunt in Cincinnati. Toni and Tonisha are their names, and they became my sixth and seventh children. April had given me a few pictures of them as babies, so I had a vision of what they looked like. I remember looking at the pictures, always thinking of how one looked just like me and the other their mom.

Years later, while in Columbus at my gym on High Street, I got a call from Jalen saying, "We found them."

I was like, "Who?"

She said, "The twins."

I got on My Space to find their pages, and the first thing that jumped out at me was my girls only lived around the corner from me and down the street from a friend of mine. This was crazy because after all these years believing the story I'd been told about them living in Cincinnati, my babies were right here. After repeated attempts to connect with my babies, I was contacted and asked to back off because their family wasn't ready for this. The folks who adopted my babies were told that the mom had had a one-night stand with a white man, and she didn't know where he was. This right here made the adoption illegal. So, when I popped up as the father, nobody knew what to do.

A few years went by without any contact until I got a ticket to their high school graduation. The first time I saw my babies was when they walked up to accept their diplomas. They both walked right past me and looked me right in the eye and didn't know who I was. I only knew who they were because of the announcer calling out their names. I stayed the whole time while my girls and their family and friends took pictures. I was so close to them that I was even in a few of the pictures without them knowing who I was.

Their adopted father and I met up and talked. He was worried about my response to this. He shared with me how the adoption happened and how April signed away the rights before the time was up for her to change her mind. To this date, my relationships with Toni and Tonisha as well as Jalen are not good. Neither twin sees me as their father but as the man who helped bring them into this world. One of my prayers was to find my girls and for them to be close. Jalen and the twins are super close, and this is all that matters to me.

Toby, the twins' older sister, and I have a close relationship now after having it be challenged and stretched. We made it through the hard part, you know, the separation, the getting to know each other, her being a teenager and my getting my life together.

It really seems like I went from having no kids to having all my children overnight. Their ages are so close together, with no more than three years separating all of them, from the oldest to the youngest. Back in 1995 when I made the decision to love me and to get my shit together for my grandchildren, I wanted to become somebody that my children could be proud of. Even if I don't have the closeness with all of my children the way I would like, I know that all my children are proud of the man I have become. I am now a grandfather eleven times and I have done an awesome job at trying to be a part of all of their lives. My goal was to give my grandchildren a shot at starting on second base. I wanted to give them a chance to go to college and have a place to stay after college with no debt.

After years of being a grandfather, I have learned there are factors that get in the way of my dreams for my grandkids, like their parents and their families. Everyone doesn't see life the way I do, and this makes it hard for me to give my grandbabies a better chance to be successful at life. I put all the eggs in a basket for my oldest grandson, Lil Damon, including a college fund, so that he could have the best shot. We started a company together, PSM Unlimited, which is a parent company to B.O.S.S. Fitness. I made him a beneficiary of my life insurance policy and my retirement account. I spent time with him talking about money and how we needed to put him in a position so that the money I leave him is for his son. Because my children started having kids so fast, it was apparent I wasn't going to have the ability to do what I was doing for Lil Damon for all of them. So, Lil Damon had to lead the way to help keep everyone on course.

After ten years and 33 percent of everything I built, it turns out that Lil Damon wasn't my son's child. His mother thought it was best for Lil Damon that he get to know his real father and his family. I haven't spoken with Lil Damon or his mother up to this point. This news ripped my heart out. I felt I needed to give Lil Damon and his family all the opportunities that I felt grandparents should.

In Closing

While finishing my book on a two-week vacation to the Caribbean, I have to say that stepping away from my life for one month has been one of the better decisions I have made. The first two weeks of my month-long sabbatical allowed me to decompress from waking up at 3:45 a.m. and working until 8:00 p.m. month on month without taking a day off. Just waking up leisurely and not having to be somewhere or have someone counting on me constantly on a daily basis helped set the stage for me to arrive on the cruise already relaxed and in a position to actually vacate my life. Not having internet or a phone for two weeks played a major role in minimizing distractions that would intervene between me and my wife. Life had taken hold of us and led to our separation. Our conversations were about our lives, the businesses, the kids, the grandkids, the money—everything but us. I can honestly say that this vacation allowed my wife and me to smile with each other again. We actually talked to each other. We laughed with each other like when we first got together. Both of us sacrificed so much to create a better life for ourselves.

You know, for the first time since this journey began, I had a chance to look back and be proud of myself. I had a chance to appreciate the hard work. And appreciate the outcome. There were times I worked so hard that I had to step outside to throw up because of exhaustion. There were times I was sick and still wouldn't take time off because the goal was bigger: I had folks depending on me. I was performing selfless acts by pushing through every obstacle. I have been able to think back on how proud I was to get my personal training certification, my first client, my first bank account at the age of thirty-five. I reminded myself how it felt to buy my first car with legit money and make my first car payment. Life got so busy, I had even forgotten about the feeling I had when I paid my first car off, when I paid all my back child support, and all the other proud moments I had during my twenty-one-year plan. In some weird way, all the small accomplishments got swept under the rug because I believed this was something that men did. Maybe I took these things for granted, or I always had my eyes on the *next* prize after completing the task at hand.

I sat on the deck most nights with my feet up, looking at the scar on my foot where I'd had surgery to repair bone spurs in my big toe from years of wear and tear. It took me back to my taking only one week off instead of the two recommended. I came back on the day of the marathon to stand on the street and high five and motivate a thousand runners with one foot propped up on a scooter. Every year since 2007, I cheer on the marathoners, staying until the last runner makes it past us on mile nine.

I had worked so hard and had so much focus on taking care of my family and the B.O.S.S. community I had lost me in the process. I forgot what makes James happy. I thought my happiness was wrapped up in my goals, my family, and my success. I found out on this getaway it wasn't. I don't know if you have ever spent so much time loving and caring about others that you forgot to love you. This is what makes me happy! I love me some me. I needed to remind myself because no one will remind you to do this: When your love is dependable, consistent, and loyal, it is hard for others to stop and see when you are hurting and in need of more. The final six months before my retirement and the completion of the twenty-one-year plan was the hardest and most challenging time in my life. I looked around. I was all alone in my business and in my personal life. Being a strong person encourages folks to always think you are ok because you don't kick and scream about the hard times. I literally looked around and saw everyone involved with their own lives. My daughter Skylar had graduated from nursing school and was working, buying a new car and a new condo. Jamie had become this successful social media influencer, putting on shows around the world, running his own business, and making money hand over fist. My son Duke was finishing up his last year at Ohio State. My baby girl Toby had become a mother and a daddy's girl, holding her life together by herself. My wife was running her business. And five of the trainers who I had mentored and helped make money had found their grooves and had their own businesses.

I had even developed a great relationship with a number of my grandkids to the point that they could call me and just say come get me, and I was on my way. And while everyone in my life had risen to impressive levels of success, they were all too busy to see I was struggling mightily. And during my struggles I was still representing to them what I represent and never cheated my family or the B.O.S.S. community.

With bags under my eyes and the weight gain, my personal struggle had hit the wall. I can't express enough how hard it was to start from the bottom, and I do mean the bottom, and rise to become a man. To whom much is given, much is required, and I always knew I had a choice either to lay down or to rise up. I never chose to run from the new level, which demanded more of me was huge for me. It still didn't mean it wasn't hard and that it didn't start to take a toll on me.

When December 31st, 2019, came, it marked something new for me. That day I retired and exhaled. I sat in my truck and let tears of joy come down because I did it. I felt I had finally become someone my children and grandchildren could be proud of. I was proud of the man I had become, proud of the way I provided for my friends and family. I was proud of how I helped others, proud of my dedication to me. Part of this feeling came from my having the feeling of being free.

For years, I kept my story and what I had been through to myself. I felt from the beginning that I needed to become a millionaire and have a ton of accomplishments before I could share my story, and I finally told my story the night of my party. The twenty-one/fifty was a celebration of completing the twenty-one-year plan and my fiftieth birthday, but more than anything, it was the last time I would be ashamed of me. The turnout was awesome, bringing together in one room people of all races and backgrounds and economic levels—all to support me. This was huge!

Folks took turns speaking about how I played a role in their lives, with my son saying he was proud to be my son. I was moved by the energy and the tears in folks' eyes when I shared my story with them and apologized to anyone who may feel I offended them by not sharing what I had been through with them. I gave everyone the ultimate understanding and asked the question, "If you had known about me going to prison, being an addict and homeless before you got a chance to know me, see me work hard, and find out I really care about each individual, would you have given me a chance?"

I can honestly say I wouldn't have done anything different. I was given a second chance at life because Lamont didn't die that day. I feel I am the luckiest man on Earth to have a wife that loves me, kids who are proud of me, and grandchildren who love their Papa. The success is icing on the cake. My father never showed me how to be a man, so becoming a better one than he was was all I had to go on. To my homeboys who felt I turned my back on them—naw, homies, it wasn't like that. I just wasn't dying in the streets or going back to jail. To members of my family who are not as close with me as we should be—it was my journey. To all the folks who supported me, who are too many to count—I appreciate you, and I believe you know that. To a power greater than myself—thank you for protecting me and moving things out of my way even if I didn't like it.

And to you for purchasing my book and supporting me, I thank you as well. I hope you are inspired by my story, and I hope you walk away with renewed energy and motivation.

Master Trainer James, out.

About the Author

James Gullatte is the author of *Results Do Matter: A Journey from Homeless to Million-Dollar Business Success* and owner of B.O.S.S. Fitness, the #1 personal training studio in Columbus, Ohio. James is also an International Fitness Professionals Association-Certified Master Trainer, Women's Fitness Specialist, Sports Nutrition Specialist, and Advanced Personal Trainer.

In 2004, James came to Columbus, Ohio, with $95 in his pocket and one goal: to help as many people as possible get fit. What he lacked in money at the time, he more than made up for in ambition. To achieve his goal, he knew he had to get his hands dirty—literally by taking a janitorial job at a gym. The rest is history. James now has over fifteen years of training experience and over 1,500 satisfied clients of all age ranges and physical abilities.

In his first book, *Results Do Matter: A Journey from Homeless to Million-Dollar Business Success*, James shares his riveting, deeply personal story journaling his rise from prison to multi-million-dollar business success. Learn more about James, the book, and B.O.S.S. Fitness at www.boss-fitness.com.